EDENDERRY
1820-1920

Popular politics and Downshire rule

D1610178

CIARÁN J. REILLY

NONSUCH

First published 2007

Nonsuch Publishing
73 Lower Leeson Street, Dublin 2, Ireland
www.nonsuch-publishing.com

Nonsuch Publishing is an imprint of NPI Media Group

© Ciarán J. Reilly

British Library Cataloguing in Publication Data.
A catalogue record for this book is available from the British Library.

ISBN 978 1 84588 596 0

Typesetting and origination by NPI Media Group
Printed in Great Britain

Contents

Foreword   7

Acknowledgements   9

Introduction   11

Agrarian unrest 1820-45   17

The Famine at Edenderry   35

Edenderry 1850-80: industry and development   43

The Land War and the Edenderry Home Rule Club   55

Literary nationalism and pastimes   77

Edenderry Town Council and the decline of Home Rule   91

Edenderry men in the 'Great War' 1914-18   101

The independence struggle at Edenderry 1916-21   109

Aftermath: Civil War and compensation   123

Snippets from the past   135

Appendices   141

Endnotes   151

Foreword

Modern Ireland continues to expand, moving at great speed as our social fabric is eroded. Local heritage, history and culture are just a few of the casualties of the marauding 'Celtic Tiger'. While economic prosperity is the only thing that those of 'my' generation have known (and welcomed), the destruction in Edenderry of many of the nineteenth-century houses, built under the patronage of the 3rd Marquess of Downshire as a measure to improve his estate, is an unfortunate consequence of this boom. While undertaking research for this study, I spoke with numerous people who shared their experiences and valuable local knowledge of what has gone before us. However, there exist many misconceptions of what actually transpired during the period 1820-1920 at Edenderry, and as such this book is an attempt to chart and record what occurred in one hundred years of Downshire rule. That it is necessary to do so cannot be overstated. Our local history is under threat from a changing society, as are our buildings and built heritage.

This book recalls the Downshire estate at Edenderry in the nineteenth century culminating in its eventual demise in the early part of the twentieth century. Important events such as the agrarian disturbances of the 1820s and '30s, the building of the workhouse and famine of the 1840s, and the development of the town by the Hill family, Marquesses of Downshire, are recalled. The town's long association with the British Army and, interestingly, the American Civil War is discussed when examining the emergence of Nationalist activity at Edenderry, spearheaded by Revd John Kinsella and George Patterson: 'Edenderry's Parnell'. In the twentieth century much of

The townhouse, built in 1823 by the 3rd Marquess of Downshire.

the activity at Edenderry concerns the Town Council and the important functions it provided for, as well as the break-up of the Downshire estate which took twenty years to resolve, following the Wyndham Land Act of 1903. The final chapters discuss the impact that the War of Independence and the Civil War had on Edenderry.

I hope this work will spark an interest in all those 'closet historians' who wish to know more about their local area, and provide a guide to those new to our community, or indeed those who have left Edenderry but for whom the 'Brow of the Oaks' is never far from their thoughts. In remembering that we must preserve our past, and be proud of what was achieved, we must also be mindful that not all of what occurred during the period 1820-1920 was glorious or noble. Certain deeds carried out in the name of Irish freedom and unity cast a dark shadow on this period. To fully understand the past we must be ready to accept this.

Ciarán Seosamh O' Raghallaigh,
Coill Blundell,
Eadon Doire,
14 Feabhra 2006.

Acknowledgements

Throughout the past year a number of people have offered valuable assistance to me in the preparation, research and writing of this study of Edenderry. To the committee and members of Edenderry Historical Society, in particular Mairead Evans and Tommy Wall, I offer many thanks for their support and advice. To Mary Carey, Sean Farrell, Padraig Foy, Eileen Hickey, Tom & Mary Julian, John Kearney, Liam Moran, Declan O'Connor, Rory O' Kennedy, the O'Kelly family, Cyril O'Neill, Antoinette Tyrell, Nan Usher, Martina and Mary at Edenderry Library, I offer many thanks. Similarly to the staff of the National Library of Ireland, the National Archives of Ireland, the Deputy Keeper of the Public Records of Northern Ireland and the Offaly Historical Society at Bury Quay, thanks is offered for their exceptional assistance.

The countless hours of conversation that I have enjoyed with Oliver Burke, a man well-versed on Edenderry's history, have been immeasurable for this project. Likewise the encouragement that Miss Mary O'Connor of the Harbour House, Edenderry, has given over many years has greatly influenced my interest in history. The academic staff at the Dept of Modern History, NUI Maynooth, in particular Professor R.V. Comerford, Professor Raymond Gillespie, Dr C.J. Woods and Dr Terence Dooley have all offered expertise and guidance during five valuable years of study there.

Without the assistance of Nonsuch Publishing, and in particular Eoin Purcell and Ronan Colgan who took this project on board, this work might never have seen the light of day. In the same way, without the support of my siblings, Garrett, Niamh, Cathal, Donal and Briain who have often listened to countless stories of Edenderry's past with patience, this book's completion wouldn't have been possible without them. And to Tara, who is always a welcome escape from the 'dusty old history books' and who is slowly becoming well-versed on all things relating to Edenderry!

Finally to my parents, Tom and Mary, to whom this book is dedicated. I offer heartfelt thanks for a lifetime of support, encouragement, friendship and love.

Introduction

In Drumcooley graveyard overlooking the town of Edenderry, beneath a huge Celtic cross lies the grave of George Patterson, known as the 'Edenderry suspect'. If Charles Stewart Parnell was the hero and 'uncrowned King of Ireland', then Patterson meant as much, if not more, to the people of Edenderry in the late nineteenth century. The headstone that the patriotic people of Edenderry had inscribed following his death in October 1891 reads, 'In grateful recognition of years given in service to his county. God save Ireland.'[1] It was his imprisonment in Kilmainham Gaol in August 1881 that had been the rallying cry of the local Land League, and the regeneration of a national ethos at the Downshire estate in Edenderry and the surrounding area. The call that rang out – '*Vive les Patterson*'[2] – helped unite the district against the oppression that existed under Downshire rule at Edenderry and under Armit, Joly and Rait Kerr rule in the nearby villages of Rhode, Clonbullogue and Castlejordan.

The death of Patterson on 23 October 1891, only three weeks after that of Parnell, came at a time when the Nationalists of Edenderry (like those around the country) were divided over the Parnell split. What had been a very strong and united body of Nationalists at Edenderry was now divided. As he had in 1881, Patterson, now in death, paved the way for the reorganisation of the party at Edenderry. Nationalist issues, in particular agrarian unrest, were very much in existence at the Downshire Estate at Edenderry throughout the nineteenth century. Despite improvements carried out by the 3rd Marquess of Downshire, the issue of rents, tenure and land ownership were the main problems in Edenderry at this time.

Celtic Cross on George Patterson's grave.

The entrance gates to Castro Petre church are an integral part of the streetscape of the town of Edenderry today. Depicting the coat of arms of the Hill family, Marquess of Downshire and owners of the 'soil' for over 130 years at Edenderry, the gates were erected in 1840. Perched at the top of the long avenue, casting a glancing eye on the everyday life of his once 'deserted village of Edenderry', is Arthur Hill, 3rd Marquess of Downshire, elegantly dressed in the robes of the Most Illustrious Order of St Patrick. Erected in 1855 by the residents of Edenderry to commemorate all that he had done to develop his estate, only time and weathering have ever posed a threat to noble Arthur on his perch.[3] Today he keeps watch on the changing landscape of Edenderry, providing a link to the past. He has witnessed many important events and has seen much change to his troubled southern estate of Edenderry.

Location

The town of Edenderry is located some forty miles from Dublin, situated in the north east of King's County (now Offaly), bordering the counties of Kildare and Meath and on the edge of the great Bog of Allen. The source

Noble Arthur on his perch.

of the River Boyne is located at Newberry pond, less than six miles from Edenderry. Throughout the nineteenth century the Grand Canal played a major part in the development of the town and its environs. The canal had passed close to the town of Edenderry in the 1790s, but a branch stretching two miles long to the town was not added until 1804. In 1780 the travel writer Philip Luckombe noted that the town of Edenderry was a 'little inconsiderable place on the edge of the Bog of Allen'.[4] Similarly, in 1817 another writer, John Gough, noted that the 1798 rebellion had greatly affected Edenderry, reducing it from a 'good town to a poor village'.[5] The comments of Charles Coote in 1801 further outline the decline of the estate when he described the 'miserable and shabby appearance' of the town with 'many houses falling to ruin' and that the town would soon 'be a heap of ruins'.[6] Writing about Edenderry at the end of the nineteenth century, Sean McEvoy notes that 'Edenderry was tucked away on the border next to Kildare, and was noted for its big market square and town hall'.[7]

Early history

The name Edenderry (Eadon Doire) derives from the Irish, 'Brow or hill-top of the Oaks', referring to the large plantation of oak trees on Blundell Hill overlooking the town. The area around Edenderry, however, was known from the earliest times as Tuath Da Mhuighe, or 'the territory of the two plains'. The Annals of Innisfallen record that in AD 859 a great battle was fought at Tuath Da Mhuighe during the reign of Malachy, High King of Ireland. The arrival of the Normans to Ireland in the twelfth century saw the area come under the control of the De Bermingham family, of whom Piers became known as the 'treacherous baron'. Many battles with the native Irish O'Connor Fhailge clan ensued and in June 1305 Piers De Bermingham killed Muircheartach Calbach O'Connor Fhailge at Carbury Castle. Seeking peace terms, Piers invited twenty-eight of the O'Connors to a feast on Christmas Day 1305 at Carrick Castle, after which he had them beheaded. This event was later cited in the Remonstrance of the Irish Princes presented to the Pope in 1317 as part of the Bruce invasion of Ireland. A prolonged siege by the Earl of Surrey in 1521 eventually crushed the last of the O'Connor strongholds at Monasteroris and the way was paved for the English plantation of the area.

In 1562 Queen Elizabeth I granted the lands around Edenderry to Sir Henry Colley as part of the plantation of Laois and Offaly, from then on known as Queen's and King's County. The area around Edenderry was then known as Coolestown, or Cooleystown, and also lent its name to the barony of Coolestown. The soil of Edenderry was, through the marriage of Sarah Colley and George Blundell, for the most part of the eighteenth century in the hands of the Blundell family who resided at the elegant Easthampstead Park in Berkshire, England. On his death in 1756, Lord Blundell left Edenderry in the hands of his three daughters. The ownership of Edenderry next passed into the hands of the Marquess of Downshire's family in 1786, when, Arthur Hill, the marquess's eldest son, known as Lord Kilwarlin, married Mary Sandys, heiress to Edenderry through her grandmother, a sister of Lord Blundell. The 1st Marquess of Downshire, Wills Hill, was elevated to the title of marquess in 1789 and died in 1793; his son Arthur then assuming the title. Heavily troubled by financial debts, Arthur died in 1801 after losing much of his place and privilege in society, including his seat on the Privy Council owing to his opposition to the Act of Union in 1800. Until 1809 the Downshire estates, which included Hillsborough and Dundrum in County Down; Blessington in County Wicklow; Clonderlaw in County Clare; a small estate in County Kilkenny; and the elegant Easthampstead Park in Berkshire, were under the control of Arthur's wife, the Dowager marchioness Mary Sandys.

When Arthur Blundell Trumbull Sandys Hill, 3rd Marquess of Downshire, came of age in 1809 he was faced with clearing the considerable debt that his predecessors had accumulated, while his mother continued to receive two thirds of the rent from the estate at Edenderry until her death in 1836.

Downshire coat of arms at
Castro Petre.

Regarded as an improving landlord, the 3rd Marquess did much to improve
Edenderry and immediately began his tenure by replacing the mud-walled
cabins of the main street with slated stone houses. He was helped in this
regard by his agents who included John and James Brownrigg, Thomas
Murray and briefly Matthew Lynge. Murray in particular was an interesting
character, as it appears that he was dishonest in his practice as agent of the
estate but was never relieved of his duties.

Agrarian unrest 1820-45

Edenderry prior to 1820

In August 1815 the then agent of the Downshire estate at Edenderry, James Brownrigg, wrote to the marquess at Hillsborough outlining the condition of the town of Edenderry and indeed all of his lordship's 14,000 acres at Edenderry. The detailed account provides us with an excellent starting point whereby to assess the Downshire estate from 1820-1920. Reporting that the Downshire estate was 'fast approaching a crisis' where every effort was being tried on Brownrigg's part 'to ward off as much evil as possible'; all was not well at Edenderry. The only measure that Brownrigg could see possible was to 'turn out the miserable beggars' who had not paid their rent. Further describing Edenderry he adds that 'here is no yeomanry – no agricultural capitalist' just peasantry and poverty.[8] Brownrigg died in 1817 from the epidemic of cholera, which affected Edenderry and added to the plight of the poor. Matthew Lynge, his successor, only served a year as agent before Thomas Murray replaced him in 1821.

During much of James Brownrigg's tenure as agent, his brother-in-law from Queen's County, Lancelot Crosadaile, was employed as a sub-agent and was unsuccessful in his application to replace Brownrigg when he died. Henry Whittaker, a substantial farmer, also acted as a sub-agent of Brownrigg between 1817-19, but later fell foul of Thomas Murray when he incurred large arrears on his holding. Relief was constantly provided for the poor such as in June 1817 when Brownrigg appointed a committee to make a list of all families in distress. A total of 100 families from the bridge

Pig Fair at
Edenderry, early
1900s.

at Cush to the church of Killane were to receive relief.[9] The Marquess of
Downshire also initiated a programme of drainage and reclamation of land
to help those who wanted to improve their holdings, appointing William
Cope to oversee its implementation.

   At pains as to how to rectify the growing discontent and poverty at
Edenderry, Brownrigg asked the marquess, 'What is to be done with such a
tenantry?'[10] The labouring class at the estate were 'starving in the midst of
plenty' and were beginning to become agitated as the cutting of the Grand
Canal at the Blundell Aqueduct in February 1816 indicated.[11] Even tenants such as the former yeoman, Mr Walsh, a tenant since the days of Lord
Blundell, could not find the money to pay rent and arrears and was to be
ejected from his holding.[12]

   In November 1815 John Greer gave testimony against James Delaney of
Drumcooley, who after failing to pay arrears owed to the marquess had all
his crops and animals brought to the pound at Edenderry. Delaney, however,
armed with some 200 men proceeded to the pound where they warned
Greer not to interfere as they loaded the crops onto Edward Rooney's boat.
Having sent for Greer, Henry Whittaker observed Delaney and his brother-
in-law Maurice Walsh herding off the cattle from the pound at Colgans
Bridge. Later that month the Marquess of Downshire and the Dowager
marchioness issued a notice to their tenants that anyone caught participat-
ing in such activities would be severely punished.[13]

   The threat of ejection from their holdings did not deter the tenants on
the Downshire estate from unlawful activity. According to Brownrigg 'the
people are as wickedly inclined as in the year 1798' and that the nightly cutting of the canal made it necessary to station armed patrols at the Downshire

bridge and at the Blundell Aqueduct. People were afraid to travel by road to Carbury and Johnstown after several mobs plundered carts and sacks of flour from people at Coneyboro when they were returning from the market at Edenderry in April 1817.[14] Despite the prevailing sense of despair visible in Brownrigg's letters to the marquess, efforts were made to employ local people in repairing the roads and town parks. Brownrigg initiated another scheme of planting Scotch fir, larch, oak, alder, birch and black poplar trees so that in the future Edenderry would be a place well supplied with timber.[15]

A dispensary was established in 1818 to provide 'charity solely for the relief of those of the really necessitous'; committee members were to carefully recommend those who they believed worthy of such help. The dispensary was under the chairmanship of Charles Palmer of Rahan House with John Brownrigg acting as secretary. Other committee members included the Marquess of Downshire, John Wakely of Ballyburley, Revd William Wakely of Monasteroris House, Revd Henry Joly, Revd James Colgan, Matthew Lynge, Humphrey Bor of Ballindoolin House, Shawe Cartland of Leitrim House, Adam Tyrell, John White, William McMullen and Robert Astle. The committee, which met on the first Tuesday of the month, appointed a surgeon to visit outpatients. The area covered by the Edenderry Dispensary included all of the Marquess of Downshire's lands in King's County, Lord Harberton's estate at Carbury, the village of Rhode, Ballyburley and the Greenhills estate and as far as Ballyboggan Bridge on the County Meath border.

Schools & buildings

In 1815 the 3rd Marquess of Downshire gave Fr Dempsey a site of one acre and fifty guineas towards the cost of building the Roman Catholic Church at Killane, while the Methodists were granted permission to construct a meeting house at the mount in 1822. However the marquess gave a greater contribution to the Protestant school, which was built on the church walk to Castro Petre providing for 120 children. It was built at a cost of £159 and had twelve desks, and in 1823 was under the guidance of James and Elenor Allen. Towards its maintenance Downshire gave £10 annually. Other schools in the area at this time included that set up by Revd James Colgan also in 1823, which catered for twenty-three Catholics and six Protestants. The stu-

Killane Church, built
in 1815.

Castro Petre School,
built *c.*1823.

dents were taught in a private house by James Philan, a native of Kilbeggan,
until 1835 when a new boys' school, known as St Joseph's, was built. The
subjects taught by Philan included reading, English grammar, arithmetic,
bookkeeping, Latin and geography while 'no attempt is made to alter the
religion of the pupils'. In January 1837 Revd Colgan organised a 'Ball and
Supper' to help alleviate the costs of the new building. The dignitaries at the
dance included John H. Nangle, High Sheriff of Kildare, John H. Walsh, Dr
Michael Gilligan and Henry Cassidy.

In 1824 a school at Coneyburrow (Coneyboro) catered for twenty-five
pupils, seventeen of whom were Catholics and taught by the master John
Wyer. A similar school was started in 1818 at Drumcooley by James Delaney,
a farmer who built the thatched and clay-walled, one-room building.
Michael Somers, who was from Eglish in the south of the King's County,

Interior of the Quaker
Meeting House.

taught the lessons. The Society of Friends (Quakers), numerous at the
Downshire estate, were also providing for the education of the children of
the area. In August 1801 John Taylor, from Ballitore County Kildare, and his
wife began a school which catered for eighteen children, six days a week.

The Market House was first proposed in 1791 by Downshire's then agent
the erratic John Hatch. The high price of provisions and the impact of the
1798 rebellion meant that the building of a suitable tholsel and market
house was postponed and was not completed until 1826. It was built by the
architect Thomas Duff and cost £5,000. In the lower storey of the house
agriculture produce was traded and traders paid a toll on each product.
Describing the Market House in 1837, Thomas Murray, stated that:

> The town hall is decorated with five arches and the orchestra is finished with
> a drawing of the King's arms and fine crown fixed over it. I have made a point
> that none of the common people are to be admitted, if they don't pay, as they
> would do harm to the floor and the walls.[16]

Blundell House was built in 1813 by the then agent of the estate James Brownrigg. It was home to the agents of the Downshire estate for the rest of the family's tenure and during the War of Independence was occupied by the British Army as a military barracks. Writing to the marquess in October 1814, Brownrigg noted that at Blundell House they were still not clear of the carpenters, who were still at work, but that they 'will soon be able to promise your lordship good accommodation when ever you will honour us with a visit'.

Agrarian unrest 1820-40

In 1824 the entry in *Pigot's Directory* recorded that in Edenderry:

> The woollen trade was formerly carried on to a considerable extent, but within these few years' unfavourable changes have taken place. At present its principle trade is in corn. Besides the chapel the Catholics possess a handsome chapel, the Methodists and the Quakers also have places of worship. The town has been much improved within these few years; most of the thatched cabins have been taken down and replaced with good stone built and slated houses. The population of the town and neighbourhood in 1821 was 1,439.

The population of the Parish of Edenderry (which included Rhode and Croghan as they were united until 1856) taken in August 1826 by Revd James Colgan, offers another perspective about the population of the area at the time. The figures given by Colgan show that there were 3,838 Catholics and 606 Protestants living in 789 houses. Further breakdown of these figures by Colgan showed that there were 406 scholars, of which only 79 were Protestants.[17]

However there also appears to have been much poverty in the area, Thomas Murray recording that in June 1824 'the people were extremely badly off for work, many of them cannot get more than one days work in the week and potatoes are 7*d* per stone'. Murray believed that providing work was a better option than providing food or charity for the poor. Commenting on providing work in 1824, Murray noted that he had 'a number of men employed clearing drains and forty-four women weeding flax'.[18] While a picture of stability and change emerges from Pigott's description of the Downshire Estate, a simmering discontent among the inhabitants of Edenderry lingered throughout the first half of the nineteenth century.

Blundell House, built in 1813 by James Brownrigg.

In February 1822 a magistrate laid papers before the House of Parliament stating that a house in Edenderry had been forcibly entered in the night by five men and that the owner had been 'desperately wounded'.[19] A petition of the local Justice of the Peace in Edenderry, James Brownrigg, was successful in obtaining a military station for the eastern part of the county in March 1822. He stressed that a permanent force was needed, indicating the futility of bringing military into the county only to take them out again. On 19 January 1821, *The Times* newspaper reported murder and plundering on a cargo boat on the Grand Canal near Edenderry stating that:

> Several gentlemen residing near to the spot have subscribed a very liberal reward to any persons who shall cause delinquents to be apprehended; and the directors of the Grand Canal Company have in a manner highly commendable offered £100 to the same purpose.

While it would appear that no one was safe in this time from the actions of villains and 'Rockite' men, there was a sectarian element in their actions. In 1829 it was reported that a young man in Edenderry had shot himself while loading his gun. His intended target, it emerged later, had been the son of a local Orangeman.[20] The issue of law and order was always to the fore at the Downshire estate, and the necessity of having a new barracks at Edenderry was raised in 1831. Many people proposed to locate the new barracks at the harbour, as it would increase security and also secure the canals, as the passage boats were always the target of villains near Edenderry. As early as 1812 social unrest had been evident when the bank of the Grand Canal at Edenderry was cut during the night in March 1812 in an attempt, according to the government's informant, to prevent the removal of foodstuffs from

Market House, Edenderry, with
1904 street lamps.

the area. Among the goods was grain that was to be used in the local distill-
eries. A reward of £200 was offered to find the culprits.[21]

In 1819, Col. Andrew Armstrong, sergeant of the Coolestown Corps and
in residence in Blundell House, wrote to Dublin Castle to inform them of
the contents of a letter which they had received at the barracks at Edenderry.
The letter outlined that the town of Edenderry was to be attacked and it
was posted in the hope that it would save 'a grate dale of blod'. Among
those to be attacked would be Michael Dunaghs, which it was claimed,
would happen suddenly. A clear warning was also sent to those seen as the
enemy or 'the men that fell out some time back' who would be 'shown
no mercy'. The letter ended with the prediction that there will be soon an
overturn in government.[22]

Another threatening letter of this period was served on Stephen
McDonnell in April 1829 by the 'The Liberty Rockite Boys' who, it was
claimed, would 'hogh all before them' should their orders not be adhered to.
It was alleged that McDonnell had taken land near Newtown and Cargan
that belonged to George Robinson. After McDonnell had received the letter a blunderbuss was fired into the house.[23] The local gentry were detested
as was anyone who assisted them in land grabbing and evictions. In October
1831 a notice was posted in Edenderry warning people not to take any
more bread from that 'insinuating, perpetrating, hypocritical baker, Williams
of Edenderry that so long a time has backed the Scotch tyrants, the Rait's
of the King's County unknown to his neighbours'. The notice was signed
by 'The Friends of Liberty' and warned those who didn't obey the orders
that there would be consequences.[24] According to Maunsel Longworth
Dames of Greenhills, in evidence he gave to the Devon Commission in
1845, George Rait was a Scotch proprietor and an improver in the area.

What made him detested in the area was that he had consolidated farms 'every time he could get a piece of land near him, or adjoining, he would take it, and so on by degrees'.[25]

A common occurrence was to order people to dismiss 'objectionable' individuals working in their pay; such was the case in 1820 when several people in Edenderry were ordered to do so. The Quaker Joseph Barnes was warned that one Mr Aylmer must be dismissed from his pay 'or else he shall be dealt with severely'. Similarly Michael Dunagh was ordered to dismiss Tim Moloney or 'any stranger for we will surely execute our business'. The letter was signed in July at the 'Thrashers Alley' of Edenderry.[26] Another attempt to force 'outside labour' out of the area occurred in 1827 when John Farrell was ordered to discharge his lodger or 'you will have to find a lodging elsewhere, at the next warning'.[27]

In 1831 Thomas Murray informed the 3rd Marquess that he had considered several plans and specifications for a new police barracks, which he had agreed to build. The favoured location was near the town harbour, chosen as it would increase security and allow the police access to the canal as well as being in proximity to the town. In a letter to the marquess in 1836 Murray told his lordship that the Kildare and King's County police were to be responsible for its upkeep. In November of the same year Murray requested that an additional magistrate be sent to Edenderry 'a stranger, and no party man; if such can be got'. By January 1838 he had received word that a magistrate was to be sent 'very soon'.

Catholic Emancipation 1829

The biggest achievement of Daniel O'Connell's lengthy career in Irish politics was to have the Act of Catholic Emancipation enacted in 1829. Another of the champions of reform for Catholics was the Bishop of Kildare and Leighlin, James Doyle, who signed his name J.K.L. (James of Kildare and Leighlin), from which the town's main street gets its name today. In August 1829 Bishop Doyle delivered a speech at Edenderry about Catholic emancipation, which was said to 'have made a deep impression in Ireland'.[28] In an address given in Edenderry he said he had become aware of the recent disturbances in the town caused by people wishing to 'prolong the antipathy between the victors and the vanquished between Catholic and Protestant'. He urged all to unite and pointed out that the Marquess of Downshire,

Another view
of a cattle fair at
Edenderry.

although a different religion, had always been good to the people of the
area.[29] One hundred years later Fr Paul Murphy celebrated the centenary
of Catholic emancipation, said to have been attended to by 3,000 people, in
the grounds of the Franciscan monastery at Monasteroris.

Francis Farrah: rents and leases

In 1831 Francis Farrah was sent from Hillsborough to sort out the problems
with rents and arrears that existed in Edenderry, and to provide the marquess
with an account of how Thomas Murray was performing as agent. Arriving
at Edenderry, Farrah found that Murray was absent and was residing in Sligo,
only occasionally calling to collect the rent. Nearly every lease on the estate
had lapsed, arrears were dating to 1824 and men such as Robert McComb,
the bailiff, and Michael Dunn, the toll collector, were amongst the biggest
defaulters of rent on the estate. Farrah was quick to work and wrote to the
marquess reporting that 'the town is kept very clean, and several of the poor
people's houses have been washed with lime, and I am happy to inform your
lordship that the town is free from fever'.[30] With so many defaulters it was
clear that Murray was not doing his job and suspicion also fell on Murray's
clerk, Henry Whittaker, about whom Farrah reported 'has been very atten-
tive to his business, with the least appearance of drunkenness'.[31]

  Unable to observe the country tenants' holdings, for want of practice of
riding on horseback, McComb, the bailiff, was sent to dispossess tenants
like Edward Roe of Cloncannon who owed £170 7s 9d and whom Farrah

believed was 'very tricky and not at all disposed to be honest'. The amount of arrears varied and Farrah was determined to force all defaulters to pay, from Thomas Usher of the Derries who owed £2 to the estate, to James O'Brien in Drumcooley who owed £999. When O'Brien died of cholera in 1832, his widow was forced to pay the arrears and Farrah noted that it was a considerable holding where the stock included 60 cattle, 200 sheep, 20 horses, 8 pigs, 58 sacks of oats, 38 of wheat, 40 acres of wheat and 60 acres of oats growing and a machine that could thresh 50 barrels of oats a day. A substantial landholder, Robert Jackson in 1814 was granted ninety acres of land to build an inn but had 'an unfavourable character with the people of the town'. Again, Murray and McComb were dispatched to farms including Jackson's to 'bring to the pound every hoof on the land, for to suffer them to go unpunished would destroy the estate altogether'.[32] Expressing surprise at being pressed for rent, Jackson informed Farrah that he was an improving and good tenant.

During the 1798 rebellion, Pilkington Homan of Shean resided at a townhouse of the 2nd Marquess of Downshire at Edenderry and frequently informed his lordship of the disturbances in the locality.[33] Heavily in debt by 1832, Farrah described him as a dishonest and 'shuffling kind of a man' but allowance was made for some of his debt as Murray had mapped fourteen acres of bog incorrectly as good land. The income from rents received while Farrah was at Edenderry on two occasions between 1831-32 reduced the deficit, despite the fact that tenants' money was often handed back if the full amount was not to be paid. On one occasion Farrah noted how Richard Shannon, later a cess collector for the estate, sent a little boy to the market house to pay his rent but that he refused to take the sum of £110 as it was £9 short.[34] Acting on the marquess's orders Murray was reprimanded for the practice of sending bills in half notes to Hillsborough meaning that there was a delay in lodging them in the bank. Problems of law and order were also expressed in Farrah's letters to the marquess, with McComb, the bailiff, said to be taking the law into his own hands. On one occasion McComb 'gave Mooney a beating, who is a notorious bad character and the people of the town thought he had only got which he deserved'.

Cattle Fair *c.*1910.

Abolishing the tithes

The question of tithes and payments of rent was a major debate in the 1830s, the inhabitants of Ballymacwilliam clearly unhappy when they petitioned the House of Lords in 1831 against the 'present system of levying tithes and the extortionist charges'.[35] What is notable about this petition is that both the Catholic and Protestant inhabitants signed it. In 1834 Downshire set about abolishing tithes, a move that was welcomed by all at Edenderry. He was entitled to collect 15 per cent from his tenants, and then pay the clergy 10 per cent and the difference he was to keep for 'the trouble of collection'. His agent at Hillsborough, John Reilly, stated that giving up the tithes was 'some small sacrifice to himself'.[36] On this occasion Downshire undertook to pay the clergy on his estates tithe compensation owed to them.

The 1834 Poverty Enquiry

The 1834 Poverty Enquiry underlined the plight of the labourers at the Downshire estate, about whom Joseph White commented that their 'mode of maintenance puzzles everyone expending a thought on the subject'. According to White, the better class of labourers in Edenderry could boast a bed of chaff and rushes. In Ballyburley, Francis L. Dames wrote that the people of the area were in a state of pauperism for the want of employment, the minute division of the ground they hold and the extravagant rent they pay for it. Dames added that:

Pig Fair at
Edenderry, early
1900s.

> The Irish peasant will promise any rent, however exorbitant, to get possession
> of a house and garden and will live in the most abject poverty to try and pay
> for it; they are thus greatly preyed on by the small farmers on these estates
> where a most careful attention is not exercised to prevent division of land.

In Clonsast, also in the barony of Coolestown, the area was noted to be
remarkably peaceable:

> …until the last two years or so, when the agitation of the Reform question,
> and the many violent speeches and publications uttered at that time, give
> rise to certain wild notions as to the right of interfering with vested rights,
> meddling with the setting of land, wages of labourers, and even domestic
> arrangements.

The correspondent to the enquiry from Clonsast noted that 'crimes of the
darker dye were not only unknown to the oldest inhabitant, but there was
even no record of their having been perpetrated in this neighbourhood
until last year, when one savage murder, besides some unsuccessful attempts
at assassination, took place'.

Murray as agent of the estate

As agent of the Downshire estate at Edenderry, Thomas Murray's handling
of affairs was questionable, while suspicion about his financial dealings lingered throughout his time there. In 1837 Downshire was alerted to this

matter and wrote to Murray asking him to ask himself 'was he an honest man'. His brother John, agent in Blessington, denounced the actions of his brother saying, 'it is injurious to me for him to be a defaulter as it leads your lordship to suppose that I am in the same situation'.[37] As a result of defaulting Downshire on money from the estate, Murray lost his salary for 1838 of £350. He was not alone in cheating Downshire, as a man named De Bor, almost certainly from Ballindoolin, was dismissed as accountant for the estate in 1825 after nine years service because of what was described as 'financial shortcomings' in his dealings. Describing the agent Murray, John Reilly, agent at Hillsborough wrote to the marquess in 1839 stating that 'Murray is to go to the north in a fortnight and promises to keep to his day and hour, at which you will laugh'. Another description in 1835 stated that he was 'strictly honest and rightly intentioned but without the energy and perseverance which is necessary to enforce payment of money'.[38]

Murray was an industrious agent however, as can be seen from his dealings in November 1835 when he brought a railroad engineer to Edenderry to have a railway station built. Murray informed the engineer that 'the best level is between this town and the Hill of Clonmullen about 300 yards north of the town gardens'. His job at Edenderry was more difficult with the shortage of resident magistrates to keep the tenants in line. Appealing in 1836 for a resident magistrate to deal with the Petty Sessions, Murray stated that 'there was only old Brownrigg, eighty-seven years old, and old Grattan who was seldom present. The Petty Sessions court had become kind of a sport since Brownrigg was deaf'.[39]

While agrarian unrest prevailed throughout this period, the collection of rents and tithes proved difficult and dangerous. In 1823 Murray wrote that he found 'all sects and classes pay tithes with the utmost reluctance and that people who have to collect subject themselves to many dangers'.[40] According to Murray the tenants at Edenderry were a 'cunning and knavish population' and wrote to the marquess that 'the persons I wish to get rid of are the poorer class of farmers or rather landholders who cannot get work for their families and eat up all that the land produces so that they never have a shilling in money to meet the rent day'. While Francis Farrah had managed to reduce the arrears from £9,559 in January 1832 to £7,165 in January 1833, Murray let them slip again and by 1836 arrears amounted £11,267. The 'shuffling' Pilkington Homan still owed money in arrears in 1840 (£275) while other defaulters included Widow Mooney (£350) and the Widow Murphy who owed £363.[41]

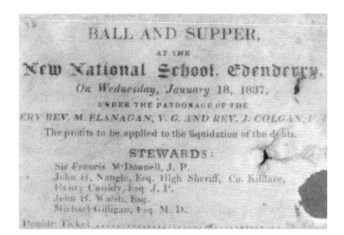

BALL AND SUPPER,
AT THE
New National School, Edenderry.
On *Wednesday, January* 18, 1837,
UNDER THE PATRONAGE OF THE
VERY REV. M. FLANAGAN, V. G. AND REV. J. COLGAN, P.
The profits to be applied to the liquidation of the debts.
STEWARDS:
Sir Francis M'Donnell, J. P.
John H. Nangle, Esq. High Sheriff, Co. Kildare,
Henry Cassidy, Esq. J. P.
John H. Walsh, Esq.
Michael Gilligan, Esq. M. D.
Double Ticket ....

Invitation to an 1837 supper ball.

Murray was delighted with the building of the Union workhouse in 1840 as he claimed it would now clear the estate of 'the crowd of beggars' that were constantly causing him problems. He was always fearful of allowing Catholics to acquire leases and thus, in 1841, fourteen Catholics were refused leases on the estate, as Murray feared they would vote for the Repeal candidates. When looking for a bailiff to replace Robert McComb in 1840, Murray asked that 'the man should be a Protestant, it will not do to have any other as the Roman Catholics all pull together and will go through any oath for each other'. When Murray was looking for the rent from the tenants in 1835 he told them 'if they could find the money for O'Connell's rent and the priest's new schoolhouse they ought to be able to pay their landlord'.

However a different side of Murray emerges from an appeal he made in 1843 to the tenants at Edenderry which he signed 'your faithful friend'. He wrote asking them to be 'punctual and regular in your dealings, till well, drain and deepen the soil, and be loyal subjects, good Christians and good tenants'. These were, in his opinion, reasonable requests as he had in the years previous provided drainage schemes, schools, farming societies and dispensaries at Edenderry.

Binns' description of Edenderry in 1837

In 1837 the travel writer Jonathan Binns gave the following description of the town of Edenderry. In his opinion, having visited the area, Edenderry was:

...a small neat town belonging to the Marquess of Downshire. Here, as well as in the county of Down, the Marquess has the character of being a good landlord. It is delightful to see the comfortable cottages he has provided for the poor of Edenderry, with small gardens in the front, and shrubs behind, and neatly painted doors and windows. They stand in one of the cross streets of the town, and the tenants pay merely a trifling acknowledgement as rent. His lordships property may generally be known by the neatness of the buildings and the taste displayed in the little praise worthy decorations which give an air of comfort and cheerfulness.42

Downshire's involvement in Edenderry

Although an absentee landlord for his entire tenure (as all the Downshire family were), the southern estate at Edenderry was always an issue with the marquess especially at election time. In 1837 he subscribed £100 to the election fund to support Mr O'Moore[43] and was vocal about the appointment of Justices of the Peace, as he was in appointing Matthew Lyne in 1818.[44] As early as 1841, Col. Lloyd of Gloster House in Shinrone, King's County had been advising the Marquess of Downshire of the activities of the disaffected at Edenderry where 'at present there is an agitation closely associated with the club at Tullamore'. Commenting on the performance of Thomas Murray as agent for the estate, Lloyd noted that Murray would 'not avail when placed against the priest (Fr Colgan) or to the crowds of the agitating people'. While the situation outlined in his letter to Downshire was worrying, Lloyd believed that 'the time may arrive when the landlord will regain his legitimate influence. The people appear to me to be tired of agitation and of acting in opposition to the wishes of the gentlemen whose neighbourhoods they live in'.[45] Others such as Edward Lucas of Springfield House, Mount Lucas kept the marquess well informed of conditions at Edenderry.[46]

A picture of how the marquess believed that the tenantry at Edenderry were on good terms with him emerges in a letter he addressed to no less a figure than the Duke of Wellington. His Roman Catholic tenants were 'in the most part respectable' and who were 'on good terms with me and satisfied'. However Downshire clearly pointed out that the clergy and their influence was the biggest threat that he faced at Edenderry. The tenants would generally vote as their landlord requires if they 'could withstand the whole power of the priesthood and the system of terror that is protected in

Main Street in the
1890s.

the country'.[47] The marquess believed that he had always acted fairly to the
tenants at Edenderry and as such he was one of a few landlords who 'possess
such respectable tenants as I do at Edenderry of the Roman Catholic faith'.
In an address to the tenants in 1841 Downshire told them that nothing
other than public duty had prevented him from admitting them to the elec-
tive franchise. However he asked what assurances he could get from them if
he gave them this privilege in times of 'political excitement'. He finished his
address by wishing them well in the dilemma that they faced between 'their
landlord and the terrorists of the day'.[48]

The Famine at Edenderry

The Workhouse

On the 6 April 1839 a meeting attended by Dr Phelan, assistant Poor Law Commissioner of Ireland, was held in the market house at Edenderry to consider the formation of a Poor Law Union in the area. The meeting was 'numerously and respectfully attended' and was chaired by Francis Longworth Dames of Greenhills.[49] The following month the Edenderry Poor Law Union was formally declared on 7 May 1839 and catered for an area in excess of 290 square miles. The workhouse received its first paupers on 19 March 1842. In his correspondence to the marquess, Thomas Murray provides us with information about the building of the workhouse. On 10 March 1840 Murray informed his lordship that he had:

> …attended this day to see the first stone of the Poor house being laid. I was called on last night by the man constructing it to inform me that the work would begin this day and he requested I would attend which I did. There was an immense crowd of the labouring class, and fifty to sixty stone masons, all waiting to be engaged in work. [50]

The running of the workhouse was overseen by a committee of elected guardians (twenty-two in total) and represented over seventeen electoral divisions which covered three counties, namely King's County, Kildare and Meath. The board also included seven ex-officios, which were mostly members of the gentry and Protestant elite.

Edenderry
Workhouse, built
in 1841.

The workhouse was erected on a six-acre site and was designed by the
Poor Law commissioner, architect George Wilkinson. It cost £5,300 and
was completed on 21 December 1841. Originally designed for 600 inmates,
during the famine it quickly catered for 1,200 people. From its inception,
the Protestant gentry such as John Ridgeway, Thomas L. Dames and John
Wakely mostly oversaw the business of the union. The Edenderry union con-
sisted of the following townlands in Kildare: Ballynadrummy, Cadamstown,
Carbury, Carrick, Cloncurry, Drehid, Dunfierth, Killinthomas, Kilpatrick,
Kilrainy, Lullymore, Rathangan, Thomastown, and Windmill Cross. In
King's County: Ballaghassan, Ballyburley, Ballymacwilliam, Bracknagh,
Clonbullogue, Clonmore and Croghan, Edenderry, Esker, Knockdrin
and Monasteroris. And in Meath there were Ardnamullen, Ballyboggan,
Castlejordan and Hill of Down. The Union covered a total area of 172,410
acres, which was valued at £95,659.[51]

   From the outset numerous reservations with the workhouse were
observed, the guardians believing that the site chosen for the workhouse
was unsuitable. Previously the site of a windmill and known as Windmill
Hill, the guardians believed that the site was exposed to the elements and
too far from the nearest pump to secure water. The guardians also believed
all materials used in its building could have been secured from local quar-
ries. However, Thomas Murray was delighted with the building of the
Union workhouse as he claimed it would now clear the estate of 'the crowd
of beggars' that were constantly causing him problems. The Marquess of
Downshire complained that the agreement for the workhouse was for £250
for four statue acres and not for four Irish acres, which was one-third less
than agreed.[52] Although the workhouse was inhabited in March 1842, the

View from the Carrick
Road corner *c*.1900.

building and the financing of the same were still causing problems in 1843
when the Guardians took their case before the Queen's Bench and tackled
the Central Commission on a technicality. The Guardians had been made
to raise the sum of £1,250 to complete the building of the workhouse as
the work carried out was said to have been 'not well provided'.[53] About this
time the Justices of the Peace for the barony of Coolestown were Jasper R.
Joly, George Rait and Thomas Murray, while the cess payers were listed in
January 1842 as John Gatchell and Richard Shannon.

In July 1843 the Marquess of Clanricarde presented a petition to the
House of Commons regarding the poor conduct of the Poor Law
Commissioners at the Edenderry Workhouse after the master of the workhouse had filed the complaint with the marquess.[54] In 1848, Thom's Irish
Almanac and Official Directory noted that the weekly cost of inmates was
£1 10s and that J.H. Nangle was chairman of the Union (E.L. Dames and E.
Wolstenholme were his deputies, with Thomas Byrne acting as clerk). The
workhouse master was one Michael Kelly, with his wife Margaret employed
as the matron. During the period 28 November 1846 to 1 May 1847 eighty-
one people died in the workhouse in Edenderry, the highest death rate in
one week being ten.

The Repeal Association and the 'Monster Meetings' organised by the
'Liberator', Daniel O'Connell, were an important feature of Irish politics
in the pre-famine days. One of his memorable meetings took place at the
Rath of Mullaghmast (the scene of the massacre of the O'Connor Fhailge
and the O'Moore of Laois in 1577), where it is recorded that many men
from Edenderry made the trip to hear O'Connell speaking.[55]

Trouble on the estate prior to the Famine

The Marquess of Downshire seldom visited his estate at Edenderry, in contrast to Blessington where it is said he visited often because of its proximity to Dublin. In September 1841 he visited Edenderry and addressed the inhabitants of the town. When the question of the 12 July riots at Edenderry was raised, Downshire told the congregation that it was the duty of every person, Protestant and Catholic, to obey the law and to keep social order.[56] Another visit was recorded in April 1843 when Mr Owen, his Blessington agent, accompanied him. The *Leinster Express* commented that 'his Lordship attended divine service at Castro Petre' and that during his brief stay, 'the Union Jack was waving from the battlements of old Blundell Castle the residence of his Lordship's maternal ancestors'.[57]

In late 1843 it was necessary for the marquess to warn his tenants against making or allowing signal fires on their farms as if they were found guilty they would be considered 'disloyal subjects and dishonest persons'.[58] The murder in May 1843 of John Gatchell, a Justice of the Peace for the Barony of Coolestown, caused outrage in the county. The *Nation* newspaper reported that he had been shot with a blunderbuss in the village of Clonbullogue while returning from Edenderry and that a reward of £100 was offered for information about his death.[59] Later that month the 3rd Earl of Rosse wrote to Downshire inviting him to a meeting that was to be held to enquire about the murder of Gatchell.[60] Gatchell, who was thirty-eight years of age, owned in excess of 1,000 acres while also acting as agent to some smaller estates in the barony of Coolestown. At the Summer Assizes at Tullamore in July 1843, one Thomas Dowling was charged with the murder of Gatchell after James Dunne had given evidence against him. Dowling, it appears, had waited for three days in bushes close to Clonbullogue in the hope of shooting Gatchell.[61]

The Famine at Edenderry

The Great Famine occurred in Ireland from 1845-53 and had a different impact in various parts of the country. One of the most important impacts it had on the town of Edenderry was the population change that occurred there from the 1841 census. During the famine it was calculated that some 1,800 persons were admitted to the workhouse, which had originally been

Statue of Arthur Hills, 3rd Marquess of
Downshire.

built for 600 inmates. Despite the lack of food that existed during the famine, it was reported in September 1845 that some ten to twenty tons of corn
had passed through Edenderry in a two-week period.[62] Writing to the Poor
Law Commissioners in 1845, Richard Grattan stated that he anticipated
'nothing short of the most widespread and destructive famine that history
has yet placed on record, unless immediate action is taken'.[63] During the
famine years the Quakers initiated soup kitchens to feed the poor and the
Edenderry guardians were unhappy with the government for failing to provide adequate assistance. The soup kitchen in Edenderry was established in
December 1846 and cost £30. The soup provided for the poor was bought
at 1*d* per quart.

In his article 'The Famine in Offaly', Tim O'Neill states that there were
34,000 fewer people in King's County in 1851 than there had been in
1841. The barony of Coolestown incorporated the parishes of Ballynakill,
Castlejordan, Clonsast and Monasteroris and with a population of 9,486 in
1841 accounted for 7 per cent of the county's population and nearly 10 per
cent of the land area. The population of the barony declined from 1841 to
1851 by 8 per cent, but some areas like Edenderry saw an increase. The town-
land of Coneyburrow was added to the town's figures in 1851, as were the

Edenderry Fever
Hospital b.1840.

workhouse figures. During the famine, the Edenderry workhouse cared for
some 14,653 people and as such was grossly inadequate for the population
of the area. The 1821 figures for the barony were given as 8,809 with nearly
6,000 of those under 30 years of age, so it was obvious the barony was experiencing population growth, as was the country on a whole. The effects of the
famine on Edenderry saw the female population drop by 2 per cent while
the male figure increased. If the workhouse figures of 1,023 were taken out
of the total parish figure of 4,884 the parish declined by 11 per cent.

A horrific picture of the impact of the famine can be seen in a story
printed in *The Times* in October 1846. The correspondent noted that a
group of trees at Ballyburley House were always full of crows. The owners of the house awoke to find the crows among the grounds reduced to
skeletons because of the hunger.[64] The Edenderry Guardians commented
during the famine that 'there is most poverty where there is least means
of getting funds'.[65] In 1846, Francis L. Dames of Greenhills was appointed
in charge of the barony of Coolestown to help relieve the suffering of
the poor. This involved the setting up of soup kitchens in the area, which
were administered by Dr Michael Gilligan, secretary of the Coolestown
Relief Committee. Dames instigated several public works such as the building of demesne walls at Monasteroris House, Greenhills and Rathmoyle.
The failure of the potato crops in 1846 and 1847 were reported to Dublin
Castle through the RIC, while Thomas Byrne of the Edenderry Board of
Guardians and Revd James Colgan applied for Indian meal to be provided

at cost price. Through Andrew Moore, a Poor Law Guardian (PLG), Colgan had applied for the building of a fever hospital in Edenderry, which he felt was as much a necessity as the provision of food.

The Devon Commission

In October 1844 John Watson of Drumcooley, who farmed 150 acres, gave evidence to the Devon Commission. He stated agriculture was improving and that the crops in the area were getting greener. According to Watson, farms ranged from five to three hundred acres and that agriculture was improving thanks mainly to the drainage works that were carried out by Thomas Murray, Downshire's agent. It is possible that Watson was misinformed about the other tenants on the estate as he also told the commission that in most cases the rent is paid well, and that there were very few people who refrain from doing so. He said that there is no more quite an area than Edenderry and that the murder of John Gatchell in 1843 was an isolated incident.

Also giving evidence to the commission was Thomas Murray, who stated that he had built cottages on the estate and was also willing to help those who wanted to build. When the tenants commit a felony, Murray stated, he had them removed, but that did not occur much as it was in his opinion a 'very quiet neighbourhood, none more quiet to be found'. Since 1820, Murray claimed that he had only evicted one tenant who had failed to pay arrears owed to the estate. Commenting on the tenant Joseph Rothery who owned a quarry on the estate, Murray stated that most of the newly built town houses were built from stone that had come from Rothery's quarry. Tactful as ever, Murray maintained to the Commissioners that he was on very good terms with the Roman Catholic tenants on the estate, and that, if he learns of anyone emigrating to America, he only relieves them of cattle to cover the cost of the rent. After twenty-three years as Downshire's agent at Edenderry, he had in his own opinion done much to change the fortunes of the town which was 'the most miserable town in Ireland' when he came. The bad land on the Rathangan road had been used to build cottages for the poor who were charged one shilling a year for them. The drainage and reclamation of land was another area that Murray was proud of. Employing an English engineer, Murray had helped local tenants drain land and he was helped in that endeavour by Lord Rosse of Parsonstown who provided financial assistance. Recalling Lord Downshire's last visit to the estate, Murray claimed that it pleased his lordship when a tenant exclaimed his thanks for the help in draining his land where 'I am now drawing corn over land where two years ago I had two bullocks drowned'.

Other local information about life at the Downshire estate, from the submissions of Robert McComb and Patrick Lacey, reiterates Murray's sentiments. McComb was a farmer tending to eighty acres on which he mainly sowed wheat and potatoes. The rotation of crops, drainage of the land and the building of slated houses, were aspects of Murray's tenure as agent that McComb found favourable. McComb suggested to the commissioners that agricultural schools should be set up so as to instruct people about improving farming methods. The murder of John Gatchell, in McComb's opinion, was as a result of him evicting tenants from Mr Gardiner's estate of which he was agent. Patrick Lacey, who farmed 108 acres at Ballyheashill, seemed content with his holding, citing the buying up of land by landlords to use for the fatting of cattle as his only major concern.

The 1848 Revolution

It is difficult to measure what impact the Young Ireland movement and the 1848 revolutions led by John Mitchell had at Edenderry. A daring escape did occur however in August 1848. On 16 August fifteen men were arrested near Trim and brought to Edenderry where they were held at Mr Pim's haberdashery shop. Among those who made their escape was Eugene Martin, a brother of J. Martin the proprietor of the *Felon* newspaper, which was the organ of the revolution.[66] The involvement of men from Edenderry in unlawful activity at this time is known, such as the case of Dr Grattan, the Chairman of the Edenderry Poor Law Union. In December 1849 the *Evening Mail* published a letter, which implicated Grattan in having attended a meeting of the 'National Alliance', a party said to have been linked to John Mitchell.[67] Many people including respectable business men in the Edenderry area were convicted in 1848 of passing forged £10 notes in the banks. Notices warning traders and banks about the forgeries were posted at Edenderry in March 1848.[68]

Edenderry 1850-80: industry and development

The 1850s

Documentary evidence as to what occurred at the Downshire estate at Edenderry in between the years 1850-80 is fragmented and sparse; only brief newspaper accounts help create a picture of the scene at this time. The papers of the Downshire family offer little information regarding Edenderry after the death of the 3rd Marquess in 1845 who died while surveying his estate at Blessington; his successors did not take the same level of interest of their estate at Edenderry. A peculiar story of interest to the Downshire estate at Edenderry is related in 1851 in *The Times* newspaper when one John Wilson (using the alias of Williams) was found guilty of trying to defraud the Marquess of Downshire at his house at Hanover Square in London. The marquess quickly realised that he was an impostor after he had presented himself as Mr Williams from Edenderry and a cousin of Dr Grattan. He had in his possession the names and addresses of other nobility and gentry, whom he hoped to also defraud.[69]

Another interesting article, which appeared in the *Leinster Leader* newspaper in March 1882, provides us with a glance at Edenderry in the 1850s, when the Edenderry Lead and Silver Mining Company undertook to mine for minerals on Blundell Hill. The venture was undertaken by a relative of Lord Downshire and a mineral engineer from Wales named Pickering (whom the locals poked fun at by calling him 'Pig-ring'). They formed the company after examining the hills around the town, and found some minerals behind Castro Petre Church. A house was built behind the church where those administering the mining

A sketch of Town
Hall, by Oliver
Connolly.

would reside. Capital for the venture was raised from investors who bought
£5 or £3 shares on allotments. The mining, it seems however, was short-lived
and many locals including Fay and Delaney lost a lot of money in the venture.
Some thirty years later, when their lands were sold for failing to meet the rent,
the correspondent in the *Leader* queried whether Fay and Delaney were entitled to repayment of their money lost in the mining swindle of the 1850s.[70]

The Roman Catholic Parish of Edenderry was re-designed in 1856 by Revd
James Colgan, meaning that Croghan and Rhode were now separate parishes. Amongst the parish priests that served in Edenderry during the period
1820-1920 were Fr Dempsey, Fr Colgan, Fr Andrew McMahon, Fr James
McDonald, Fr Michael Wall, Fr J. Wyer, Fr J. Kinsella, Fr Bolger, Fr Connolly,
Fr J. Kearney and Fr Paul Murphy. The vicars and rectors of Monasteroris
and Castro Petre during the period 1820-1920 included John Jones in 1818,
Graham Philip Crozier (1830), Henry Moore (1842), John Edward Murray
(1844), John Newcome (1883), Robert Bodel (1905) and Henry St Claire
Jennings in 1922. Appointed in 1844, Revd John Murray was a nephew of
Thomas Murray, agent for the Downshire estate and a son of John Murray,
agent for Downshire's estate at Blessington in County Wicklow.

In 1852 Lord Ashtown evicted some 700 people from his land at
Ballinowlarth, Clonbullogue, many of whom ended up in the workhouse
in Edenderry, which at this time was catering for close to 2,000 people.
Some years later many of those who had come from the Clonbullogue
and the Bracknagh area of King's County were still residing at Edenderry,

and indeed even to this day family histories can be traced back to those evicted from Ballinowlarth. When Sir Richard Griffith conducted his survey of the tenements of the area in the 1850s, these evicted families from Ballinowlarth would have been included in the Edenderry survey. Better known as 'Griffiths Valuation', every landholder in Edenderry (the parish of Monasteroris) is listed giving the acreage and value of the land, including from whom it is leased. The parish of Monasteroris included the townlands of Ballinla, Ballycolgan, Ballyhugh, Ballymorane, Clarkville, Cloncannon, Codd, Cushaling, Derries, Drumcooley, Edenderry, Eskerbeg, Eskermore, Killeen, Leitrim, Lumville, Monasteroris, Rathgreedan, Rathlumber, Rathmore, Rathvilla (or Rathclonbraken), Rogerstown and Shean. While Griffiths Valuation is primarily used today for tracing ancestry, it also provides information about landholders, houses, middlemen and the occupations of the employed at Edenderry at this time.

Men such as Joshua Manley of Monasteroris House owned over 1,000 acres of land at Monasteroris, where he sublet to tenants such as the Allens, Roches, Wilsons and Ryans. The bailiff of the Downshire estate, Robert McComb, owned 106 acres at Killane and 30 acres at Rathmore of which he sublet 13 acres to one Edward Behan. The survey of the town of Edenderry subdivides the individual streets, which included Windsor Street, Dirty Lane, Upper Coneyboro, Blundell Street, New Row, Main Street and Downshire Row. Located behind the Market Square on the Clonmullen side, Dirty Lane included ten holdings, one of which included a quarry and gravel pit. Residing on the Main Street, Arthur Keating was a gunsmith, James Dunne a butcher, Thomas Tinkler a baker and James Kennedy a tailor.

The Grand Canal

Without the Grand Canal, Edenderry in the nineteenth century would have not as prospered as it did, the canal providing a much needed communication network and transportation for goods such as peat, corn and flour to Dublin. On numerous occasions throughout the period 1820-1920, the livelihoods of the people of Edenderry were threatened when the canal burst its banks. In 1833, Thomas Murray informed the Marquess of Downshire that a massive breach in the canal at the 'Downshire' turn had 'inundated the entire country, causing considerable damage with one child drowned and several persons having narrow escapes. On this occasion one poor women and her

Last barge leaving Edenderry
in 1961.

five children had to climb on top of their house to avoid been swept away.'[71]
Another breach occurred in February 1849 between Ticknevin and the
Blundell Aqueduct, where 1,000 men were employed under Christopher
Mulvany in repairing the damage. This work was undone in 1855, when the
canal breached again with 500 men employed at twopence per day to seal
the breach. The canal was reopened in January 1856. Relief efforts when the
canal next breached in 1916 were hampered by heavy snowfalls and bliz-
zards. The canal remained closed for three months, the repairs using 25,000
tons of clay and costing more than £6,000.[72] A visiting English scientist,
observing the damage done at Edenderry in 1916, noted that an earthquake,
which was recorded in the Irish Sea at the same time, might have caused
the breach. The canal continued to be used for carrying cargo to and from
Dublin until 1961, when the last barge left the town. A major breach of the
canal occurred in January 1989, and since then considerable exertion by the
Office of Public Works (OPW) has taken place to insure that further damage is not caused to the Grand Canal at Edenderry.

The inhabitants of the Downshire estate involved themselves in more
than local issues and were quite frequently presenting petitions to the House
of Commons, such as the petition in 1856 which called for the abolition of
Capital punishment.[73] Other petitions included that of June 1863 to have
all public houses closed on a Sunday.[74] The Society of Friends (or Quakers)
at Edenderry were looking for the repeal of the Contagious Diseases Act
in 1870[75], while Sir Patrick O'Brien, MP for King's County, presented an
address of the people of Edenderry to the House of Commons in 1866 for
an amendment of the laws between the landlord and the tenant.[76]

Present-day view of the Grand Canal at the Downshire bridge.

AGENTS AT THE DOWNSHIRE ESTATE	
1799-1800	James Brownrigg
1800-1817	John Brownrigg
1817-1818	James Brownrigg
1818-1819	Matthew Lynge
1819-1850	Thomas Murray
1850-1902	Thomas Murray

Worldwide events such as the Crimean War in the 1850s influenced proceedings at the Downshire estate, as the following list of subscribers for a fund in 1855 for the Crimean War indicates. With many local men serving in the British Army at the time, funding for such a cause was widely supported. Amongst those who contributed by sending money included; Revd J. Colgan, Revd W. O'Neill, Rose Murphy, James Murphy, Mary Mooney, Pat Kelly, T. O'Brien, Pat Furey, M. Mulvin, Thomas Murray, T.R. Murray, W. Morrison, J. Fitzgerald, A. Butler, H. Gill, T. Lemon, E. Carroll, G. Reilly, R. McComb,

Capt. T. Longworth Dames of Greenhills
House *c*.1855.

W. Watson, James Dunne, James Bennett, G. Dunne, M. Dunne, P. Dunne, P.
Kennedy, M. Brerton, Dr Newcombe, John Cronly, J. Masterman and Mrs
Sheil.

One of the most influential figures in the nineteenth century was that
of Michael Paul (or M.P.) O'Brien, who, in January 1855, began one of
the most successful businesses in Ireland. With branches also in Tullow,
Allenwood, Clonbullogue, Moyvalley and Kilmeague, O'Brien's shop,
called the Universal Providing Stores (UPS), sold everything 'from a needle
to an anchor'. The site of the UPS was established in 1840 as a trading store,
O'Brien commencing business there on 10 January 1855 in a store forty
feet by twelve feet long. By 1899, the UPS, according to its trade list, had
expanded to 326,250 cubic feet. The success of his business was because 'the
people of Edenderry and the surrounding countryside are a trusting, industrious and sober people'. O'Brien was an intelligent and articulate man
with enough foresight to suggest that Edenderry was a seat suited to industrial development owing to the plentiful supply of water. Writing towards
the end of the century, O'Brien stated that it:

> …would be a pleasing realisation to again hear the tolling of the factory work
> bells, the tread of the busy workers' hurrying footsteps to their daily tasks,

UPS advertisement.

the hum of the big wheels, the click of the looms, the stroke of the hammers, the drip of the whiskey stills, the bubble of the brewery vats, and the rattle of the traffic that would indicate the revival of commercial manufacturing in Edenderry.[77]

The 1860s

The opening of the Ulster Bank in 1862 underlined the growth of Edenderry, thanks mainly to the large number of local businesses and tradesmen. R.H. Matthews was the first manager of the Ulster Bank, a post he held until 1881 when he was replaced James T. Galloghy. The branch opened on 3 March 1862 in the building that was formerly the parochial house, the last occupant being Revd James Colgan. On some occasions mass was said here as people thought the church at Killane was too far to travel in bad weather.

Despite the tenants at the Downshire estate's unhappiness with the rents and rates imposed by an absentee landlord, scenes of joy at Edenderry greeted the coming of age of the 5th Marquess in January 1866.[78] The *King's County Chronicle* reported that the 'Union Jack could be observed floating in

the breeze, and in a prominent part of the street, a monstrous bonfire entitled its lurid place'. Later in the evening a 'grand display of fireworks was to
have taken place, but this was put back until the return of the very popular
agent of the property Thomas Murray', which was regretted by all present.
The locals, it was claimed, were all vying with each other as to who would
put on the most impressive display for the marquess as the market house was
'beautifully illuminated'.[79] In 1868 the residents of the town had a memorial
obelisk erected opposite Blundell House to the memory of Arthur Hill, 4th
Marquess of Downshire who died in that year. Michael Dunne of Edenderry
was appointed High Constable of King's County in 1869, the only man from
the town to hold that position in the nineteenth century.

Population change in Edenderry 1861-1911

1861	1661
1871	1873
1881	1555
1891	1577
1901	1611
1911	2208

Administration

Located in the north east of the county, officials from Edenderry were
limited in the administration of King's County. Men such as John Wakely,
Jasper Joly and later Sylvester Rait Kerr, were amongst a minority from the
locality who offered any input into the running of the county. Directories
such as Thom's Directory offer an insight into local affairs during this
period including information about the Board of Guardians, the Royal
Irish Constabulary (RIC) and the Petty Sessions court. In 1855 Denis Hayes
is listed as being the head constable of the RIC at Edenderry, William
Kennedy the cess collector, John Hipwell the stamp distributor and Thomas
Tinkler was clerk of the Petty Sessions court which met every second
Saturday. The Board of Guardians was chaired by J. Nangle with Thomas
L. Tyrell of Clayton House as vice-chairman. Others in the workhouse

Edenderry from the
Manning Survey
1857- P.R.O.N.I.

included Edward Dowling as master, Maryanne Kelly as matron and William
Bermingham as clerk. Joshua Manley, John Thomas Hamilton and Edward
John Bor of Ballindoolin represented Edenderry on the magistrates of the
county in 1863. By 1872, William Smyth was head constable of the RIC;
Michael Dunne was the cess collector; Patrick Kelly the stamp distributor;
Charles Johnson was clerk of the Petty Sessions court; and Hugh Farrell
had replaced Dowling as master of the workhouse. Positions it seems were
held for long periods of time, although George Gill replaced Dunne as cess
collector in 1882. As land agitation and radical politics increased towards the
end of the century, Edenderry saw many changes in personnel at the RIC
barracks. In 1882 James Caulfield was head constable while others included
Macken, Barnes and, in 1906, James McMahon.

While the priests were influential and controlled the minds of the people,
at several times the inhabitants of the Downshire estate ran the wrath of
the local clergy, such as occurred in 1871 when Revd Turner PP of Rhode
compared the actions of the tenantry to that of the 'communists of Paris'.[80]
Priests of the area always made themselves available to make representations
for the people, but were, in the opinion of William J.H. Tyrell of Grange
Castle, 'the greatest drunkards and most immoral characters in their parishes'. In March 1880 a priest making representation for the able -bodied
workers of the parish, highlighted the plight of many of the ordinary tenants at Edenderry when he stated that they would 'rather eat grass or die of
starvation rather than give up their homes and go into the workhouse'.[81]

Edenderry
Railway Station.

Employment

The building of the railway line between Edenderry and Enfield from 1874-77 provided much needed employment in the locality, which was further bolstered by the arrival of Daniel and John Aylesbury, Quakers from Bristol. In 1878 Daniel Aylesbury began to work with the Williams family at the Market Square in Edenderry where they had a furniture factory and sawmills. He later married into this family and set up his own timber business, the first of which was located at the town's Market Square, before moving to a permanent location beside the Grand Canal harbour after the premises was destroyed by fire in 1888. The premises at the harbour were also destroyed by fire in 1904, causing massive unemployment in the area. Commenting on the fire of 8 June 1904, the *King's County Chronicle* stated that the fire 'spread with remarkable rapidity' before Boatman Tierney noticed the fire when passing the harbour at midnight. A huge crowd of locals gathered and feverishly tried to put out the fire by drawing water from the canal. Directing the crowd were the District Inspector Irvine and Head Constable Hughes of the RIC. The damage caused was estimated at £30,000, only weeks after Daniel Aylesbury had declined to have the mill insured with a fire insurance company. *The Chronicle* commented that it was a sad occasion for Aylesbury, who employed over 150 people, and that the machinery used in the mills was the most modern and best of its kind in the world.[82]

A concrete factory replaced that destroyed in 1904, and Aylesbury thrived until 1932 when it eventually closed. Handcrafted goods, these wooden

Aylesbury's Mills.

tables, chairs, carts etc. were sold the length and breadth of the world including at the St Louis Exhibition. Other businesses included D.E. Williams's bakery and grocery shop and Moran's Coach factory. Another form of employment between the years 1854-60 was that provided by the Boyne drainage at Kishawanna, which was supervised by Thomas R. Murray. Many stone, bronze and iron artefacts were found, with which Murray opened a museum in the market house. He would later sell these items and more to Cambridge University in 1900.

The Dames estate at Greenhills consisted at this time of 1,000 acres and employed twenty-six workmen on the estate who were each paid 9d per day. The house staff consisted of a butler, a footman, a coachman, cooks, parlour maids, a chamber maid and a caulry maid. Similarly, the Beaumont Nesbitt estate at Tubberdaly provided employment for forty servants who were housed in some twenty houses on the estate.

In 1877 a branch of the Midland and Great Western Railway was built between Enfield and Edenderry, linking the town to the main Galway-Dublin route. Miss Downing Nesbitt of Tubberdaly House provided £10,000 towards the cost. The Nesbitts regularly took part in cattle shows in Dublin where their pedigree Aberdeen Angus would be on display. It was for this reason that she financed the railway line, which became known as the Nesbitt Junction line. The work on the line had commenced in 1874 when provisions to buy the necessary land were put in place after the Company's Bill had passed through the House of Commons. Evidence that a new business class at Edenderry had been established at this time can be seen in the representatives from Edenderry who made up the members of

Greenhills House,
home of the Dames
family.

the King's County Jury at the Winter Assizes in December 1879. While T.L.
Dames, Henry C. Joly, John Charles Smith and Garrett C. Tyrell represented
the gentry; shopkeepers such as Patrick Fay, Joseph and Patrick Mulvin
and the local hotel keeper Peter Delaney represented the growing business
community at Edenderry.

The Land War and the Edenderry Home Rule Club

'Edenderry's Parnell'

The morning of Tuesday 2 August 1881 was no ordinary day in the town of Edenderry. At 9 a.m. more than 3,000 turf carts lined the road which led out of the town to the village of Rathangan in County Kildare. The *Leinster Leader* reported that it was 'the most important celebration ever seen in this country'.[83] Branches of the Land League from Mullingar, Tullamore and 'historic Bodenstown' had come to support George Patterson, a local man who had been arrested the previous week and imprisoned in Kilmainham Gaol.[84] The emergence of Nationalist politics at the Downshire estate can possibly be traced prior to this day, but a national ethos was copper-fastened on that day as the crowds assembled in a jovial mood to draw home the turf of Patterson from the bog. This accelerated the general demise of the Downshire estate and with it the decline in fortunes of the local Protestant ascendancy. The Nationalists at Edenderry began to mobilise, educate and assert themselves under the banner of Home Rule. The push for Home Rule, which dominated Irish history from the 1880s right up to the end of World War I, provided the political and social training for the Nationalists at Edenderry who would later govern themselves once the Free State was established in 1922.

Like many others of the time, Patterson had served his time in the British Army, having fought in the Punjab in 1848-49. It was during his army career (1840-53) while in India that he was wounded with a poisonous arrow, an injury that affected him for life. He was compared to the Fenian

John Boyle O'Reilly, for whom, like Patterson, 'a soldier's coat could never conceal his love for Ireland'.[85] Having left the army, Patterson was employed in the Colonial Office of the Australian government before returning to Edenderry after the death of his brother to run the family business and take care of the land. The Patterson family had owned a public house in Edenderry since 1821 and were well-respected members of the community. He was quickly under the watchful eye of the RIC, who saw his powerful presence and oratory skills as a problem in the locality, as law and order were deteriorating as Nationalist politics established itself at the Downshire estate.

On 21 June 1881, after attending mass at 6 a.m. in Edenderry, Patterson was arrested under the Coercion Act, which had been introduced by the government to curb the actions of the Land League.[86] Despite his social standing in the community and his previous army career he was singled out as the only arrest on that day in Edenderry; 'Thus England honours those who fought her battles well', commented the *Leinster Leader*.[87] The government report on his arrest stated that since 30 September 1880 he had been under surveillance and was guilty of writing threatening letters and promoting 'boycotting' in the area.[88] He was taken to Kilmainham Gaol on the 9.30 a.m. train and was greeted on his departure by a large group of sympathisers whom it was said, 'had sprung up out of the ground'.[89] The Revd John Wyer prevented a collision with the police and maintained that the best way to honour Patterson was to look after his business. The police were 'hooted and groaned' as they performed their duties throughout the day. Among those gathered at the station included some of Patterson's friends including Terence O'Kearney White, a solicitor; Henry Pelin, the postmaster; T.H.F. Bor of Ballindoolin; Patrick Fay and Michael Paul O'Brien, prominent businessmen. As an act of the defiance the Home Rule band paraded through the town playing Nationalist tunes.[90]

The arrest of Patterson proved to be a turning point in the fortunes of the local Land League and the Home Rule party, and tactics adopted elsewhere in the country were soon adopted at Edenderry. Huge crowds of Land Leaguers blocked sheriff sales of farm animals at Carbury and Castlejordan in June 1881. A feature of the day was how well the branches in Carbury, Edenderry, Rhode and Castlejordan worked together to defy the landlords and their agents. In Edenderry following Patterson's arrest, postcards were distributed to the shopkeepers of the town, which named people who had been 'boycotted' warning them from supplying goods to such people.[91] The

The Patterson family
*c.*1900.

RIC was also active throughout the summer of 1881, when they raided the homes of Catholics in Edenderry checking to see if men were in their beds at night. One such raid occurred on 24 July when Constable Gibney visited James Gray, a local blacksmith and the RIC, 'it is said thought to actually intrude into his wife's bedroom'.[92] Another man named Crowley, who owned a flour store, was also interrogated by Sub-Constable Shankey. The correspondent for the *Leinster Leader* believed that it was 'a mockery to talk about Russia when one sees what is going on here'.[93]

The land surrounding the Downshire estate was also owned by members of the Protestant ascendancy who were every bit as detested by the people as the Downshires were. These estates became legitimate targets of the Land League and, in later times, more militant Nationalists. By 1922 those such as Wakely of Ballyburley House, Rait-Kerr of Rathmoyle House and Beaumont Nesbitt of Tubberdaly would be attacked and burned, their owners driven from their lands never to return to the locality. Another person who owned land in the locality was a Mr Armit at Castlejordan, which straddled the county border of King's County and Meath. The land agent, Garrett Tyrell of Ballinderry House in Carbury, administered many estates including that of Armit's. In July 1881 Tyrell brought about an eviction on behalf of Armit of William Carew at Castlejordan. A huge demonstration was organised by the Land League under the auspices of Edward Wyer, a poor law guardian, where it was estimated that four to five thousand people gathered to hear speeches. As with the demonstration at Carbury earlier in the month, the Land League goat was paraded at the sale carrying the slogan, 'I have come here before you all; by the Land League to stand and fall, I'm always willing I do say, a just and proper rent to pay. But as long as horns grow from my crown, rack-rents I'll keep pucking down.'[94]

Revd John Wyer *c.*1881.

The Edenderry brass band attended on this occasion at Castlejordan, where Mr Furey carried a banner proclaiming 'Union is Strength'. The sale was opposed by Terence O'Kearney White and Matthew Moore bought the cattle for Carew at a price of £13 1s. Revd John Wyer of Edenderry addressed the assembled crowd on this occasion, warning that ' the day will come when the landlord will be driven bag and baggage out of Ireland'.[95] The only way that landlordism could be brought to its knees, Wyer maintained, was to 'continue to carry out agitation in a constitutional manner' and that 'King's County will always occupy a van in the Land League until bad landlordism was banished like St Patrick banished the serpent'.[96] At Castlejordan in late July, Michael Costello of Ardbash House, Edenderry told the crowd that the 'people of Edenderry were even more determined' to assert their rights after the arrest of Patterson. This is what transpired a few days later when on 2 August 1881, the local people assembled to bring home from the bog the turf of George Patterson. This was a symbol of defiance, a recruiting drive and a mobilisation showing the landlords and the RIC that the Land League at Edenderry was a force to be reckoned with.

At 9 a.m. on 2 August 1881, 3,000 carts assembled along the Rathangan road out of Edenderry, led by the Edenderry Land League which consisted of 830 carts. The procession was headed by a group of small boys dressed in green and mounted on donkeys. The Land League piper Davy Woods provided the music. The influence of the clergy can be seen in the refusal of

T.F. O'Toole.

John Delaney's offer to supply barrels of porter for those helping to draw the turf; no drink was allowed as Revd Wyer wanted to maintain the peace and carry out the proceedings in a dignified manner.[97] The RIC was not needed on this occasion, owing to the good behaviour of the people. It is interesting to note that there were only six policemen on duty that day when it appears that the number stationed at Edenderry was a lot more. The necessity to have such a large police presence in the area was emphasised when on 22 July 1881, forty RIC were called from Edenderry to Portarlington, to help with the sale of farm animals from an evicted tenants' land.[98]

The local businessmen rallied to the occasion of drawing home Patterson's turf and some, like Eugene O'Brien of Leitrim House, provided carts that were 'freshly painted and drawn by the finest horses'. The banners that were carried indicated the feelings of the local Land Leaguers displaying quotes such as, 'Temperate but firm resistance to oppression' and 'When Irishmen are united who can withhold their rights.' The evening concluded with a visit to the grave of Revd Mogue Kearns and Col Anthony Perry (Wexford rebels hanged on Blundell Hill in 1798 and buried in Monasteroris graveyard), where 700 men from Rhode and 350 from Carbury joined them.[99] The Nationalists of the area had prior to this, in 1874, erected a huge Celtic cross over the grave of the Wexford rebels and the place had become a place of pilgrimage for Nationalists.

Citing Patterson's army record as proof of his character, Timothy

The village of Rhode,
*c.*1900.

Healy MP highlighted his imprisonment during a debate in the House of
Commons. One week later he was released from Kilmainham and given a
magnificent reception in Edenderry. The people of Croghan had elected
him to their electoral division during his incarceration. Twenty years previous, in 1861, the people of Croghan had done the same for a relation
of Patterson, Myles McKeon of Edenderry, who was similarly ostracised
from his holding.[100] Another of the local 'suspects', Bernard Ennis of Rhode,
supplied his land to be used for a demonstration on 9 August 1881, which
coincided with the release of Patterson. A bonfire was lit on Leitrim Hill
between Edenderry and Rhode where an effigy of Norris Goddard (who,
having bought up the land at Croghan, was detested in the area) was burnt
to the great delight of the crowd. It was claimed that two policemen who
were hiding in the trees at Leitrim had seen the burning which was reported
to the RIC at Edenderry.[101]

   With the suppression and outlawing of the Land League branches, the
ladies of Edenderry rallied to continue the cause should the police put a
stop to Nationalist activity in the area. The ladies formed their own branch
of the Land League at Edenderry in November 1881, and its progress was
due mainly to the efforts of Mrs J. Moore, Mrs Letty O'Toole, Mrs Byrne
and Miss Brophy. The women sarcastically maintained that the reason they
had not received any attention from the RIC was because Head Constable
Macken was still a bachelor. In their opinion he was 'an awfully nice
man'.[102]

Letty O'Toole, with her mother and three children.

'Battle of the Tolls'

The so-called 'Battle of the Tolls' was another important victory for the people of Edenderry over the system of landlordism that they had come to despise. On 4 November 1881 a local man named William Killaly refused to pay the tolls at the weekly market, which was owed to the 5th Marquess of Downshire. So important was the occasion that Killaly was to be presented with a horse in recognition of his stance. No longer would the women of Edenderry fear having their clothes ripped from them 'to see if they had eggs, food etc. underneath'.[103] The marquess responded by sending five bailiffs to the market the following Saturday to try and collect the tolls, even stationing himself at the window of the town hall to supervise. On this occasion, thanks to Killaly's defiance, the people laughed and sneered at the bailiffs. The times had changed from when the people, it was said, would tremble 'when they heard the sound of footsteps from Blundell House'.[104]

Arthur Hill, 5th Marquess of Downshire.

The Edenderry Home Rule Club

The Edenderry Home Rule club was the 'most durable club in the county' according to Gerard Moran.[105] It was comprised mainly of farmers, shop-keepers, publicans and journalists. Like many of the other clubs and societies membership overlapped, as the officers of the Home Rule club comprised members of the Board of Guardians from Edenderry Workhouse and later the clergy. Men such as Michael Costello (secretary), Charles Jellico P.L.G. of Ballycolgan (vice-president), Edward Wyer of Killowen (President) and Henry Pelin (treasurer) were the influential figures in the club's formation. Later, men such as George Patterson, Revd John Wyer, Revd John Kinsella and Revd Connolly played important roles in the club's success. The *King's County Chronicle* cites the first meeting of the club in January 1876 when Michael Costello acted as chairman in Keown's Hotel, where they met.[106] However, the *Leinster Leader* newspaper suggests that the club may have existed some ten years previous to this. In November 1881 Head Constable Macken raided a meeting of the club and claimed that they were holding an illegal Land League meeting. The members informed Macken that it was the Home Rule club and invited him to view their minute book which 'is a faithful minute book since our inception in 1866'. With justification Macken was told that, until the government declared them an illegal group, they had a right to meet.[107]

The Home Rule club in Edenderry drew upon its members from the surrounding district as well as from the counties of Kildare, Meath and Westmeath. The membership quickly rose from 216 members in 1876 to 366 in 1877, and was to the forefront of all political issues in the county. The club had as a member the Kildare MP, Charles Meldon, who joined in September 1876, but the parliamentary representatives for King's County, Sir Patrick O'Brien and David Sherlock, never joined, something that angered the local branch.[108] It was the frustration felt by the misrepresentation of the county by these two MPs that led the Edenderry Home Rule club to develop into a strong entity serving the interests of the locality. In February 1877 Sherlock was severely reprimanded by the club for failing to attend the annual conference of the Irish Home Rule party in Dublin and was said to be 'totally unworthy of the trust placed in him as one of our county's representatives'.[109] Neither O'Brien nor Sherlock had attended the demonstrations held in Edenderry in late 1876 and 1877.[110] Among those who spoke in Edenderry in the early days of the Home Rule club was Isaac Butt, founder of the Irish Home Rule party, who attended a demonstration on 17 September 1876.[111]

The radical and obstructionist policies supported at national level by Charles Stewart Parnell and Joseph Biggar were also supported by the Edenderry club who argued that if the obstructionists were encouraged then 'the government would not treat Ireland with contempt'.[112] The club also believed that O'Brien was unworthy of his position and resolved in August 1878 that 'we consider the reported speech of Sir Patrick O'Brien lately at Philipstown unworthy of a representative of the King's County' and that any views that he expressed were not a reflection of the views of the electors.[113] Upon a proposal by Charles Jellico in September 1877 the club began to consider the idea of contesting the election with a local representative, such was their frustration with their MPs.[114] By 1880 Sherlock had resigned from politics and the club had already begun to show support for another candidate, Bernard C. Molloy, who was a member of their club. He had written to the club in August 1878 seeking their support in his candidature for the next election, and a six-man committee was appointed to meet with him.[115] Among the interests that Molloy agreed to champion were matters of an extension to the franchise, amnesty for prisoners, reform of the grand jury and obstruction to parliament business. In March 1880 the club adopted that O'Brien and Molloy would be their candidates. The idea of proposing a local representative to stand in the election had subsided with Costello arguing that there was not much need for one at the time.[116]

The current issues of the day were widely discussed by the club's members who resolved in 1880 that all party members should sit on the opposition benches in the House of Commons. The club were among the first to support Parnell for the leadership of the party, stating that he 'had displayed all the qualities which are essential for the position'.[117] Many of the Home Rule club were also part of the league that began in 1881 to establish better housing for the tenantry, calling themselves the Edenderry House League. This club included figures such as Costello, William Moran and Padraig O'Kennedy.[118] The Home Rule club used every opportunity when the political climate reached boiling point to showcase its strength as they did with great effect on St Patrick's Day 1881, much to the annoyance of the Unionist neighbours. On the evening of St Patrick's Day, the Home Rule brass band, conducted by a Mr Murphy, made a tour of the town playing Nationalist tunes and carrying Home Rule banners.[119]

Unionist response and Poor Law Union Politics

Alarmed at the growth of the Home Rule club and Irish National League branches in Edenderry, the Unionist and Protestant landowners rallied to maintain their Union with Great Britain, but more importantly their own interests. The rallying cry of the southern and northern Unionists was 'Home Rule is Rome Rule', and where land, privilege and money were concerned, the Protestant elite were determined to oppose the creation of a parliament in Dublin. At their height of power during the 1880s they would slowly begin to see their influence wane and by 1923, and the end of the Civil War, most of the influential landlords in the vicinity of Edenderry were selling up their holdings, having been intimidated from the land.

As land agent for the Joly estate at Clonbullogue, the Armit estate at Castlejordan and the Grattan estate in Co. Kildare, Garrett Tyrell was both hated and revered in the district. Hated by the Home Rulers and the tenantry that he evicted from the land, he was revered by the Unionists as a staunch defender of their interests. In his role as land agent he was in an ideal position to comment on the Nationalist movement, and indeed offers a unique insight on these events from a Unionist perspective. Writing to a special commission in 1888, set up to investigate the activities of the Land League, Tyrell records that before the establishment of the Land League that 'Edenderry was a very quite peaceable place and rents on the whole were paid even in 1879 which was a bad year'.[120] According to Tyrell the real trouble began in 1881 when 'there was a general strike against the rent in the district and there were several outrages'.[121] A branch of the Land League at Castlejordan superseded that of Edenderry, and indeed membership often overlapped, such as was the case with Edward Wyer and Charles Jellico. Up until 1881, rental payments were very good and often the tenants would crowd the market house in Edenderry in such a way that it proved difficult to keep them out.[122] The Protestant landowners of the locality met in Edenderry in November 1881 to discuss the seriousness of the Nationalist agenda, which was threatening their ascendancy. The tenants of Edenderry were described by Dr Jasper Joly as being a 'pestiferous society', and he called for a Defence Association to be formed to protect their holdings. Speaking to this meeting, Dr Boylan of the Dublin Stock Exchange spoke of the need for them to unite and protect their interests, calling on all members of the business class to do so at once.[123]

In his submission to this special commission in 1888, Tyrell maintained that the Land League had used the threat of violence to prevent tenants from paying the rents owed to the landlord. One man named Hickey from Clongall near Castlejordan feared paying, even though he found the rates favourable. Hickey had told Tyrell that he was willing to pay the court fees of over £10, which he would face if the issue were settled in the courts. This, Hickey believed, was a more convenient measure rather than to face the wrath of the local Land League. Likewise in May 1881, Thomas Conlon of Carrick had informed Tyrell that at a meeting the previous Sunday, at which Fr Kinsella of Edenderry was in the chair, tenants were warned that they must withhold payment.[124]

The landlords and their agents lived in fear of attack and reprisals against them. The Tyrell brothers of Ballinderry and Grange found it necessary to have an armed guard employed at their lavish country homes; such was their reputation in the locality. The soldiers stationed there also performed the task of removing crops from boycotted lands. At Grange Castle, which at this time housed a museum, the pots and pans of the soldiers now replaced important artefacts that the museum once held.[125] The aforementioned Norris Goddard, whose effigy had been burned at Leitrim, and Mr Ormsby of Newberry Hall found it necessary to carry revolvers when they

Newberry Hall, Carbury.

visited Edenderry on business.[126] These fears were genuine and in May 1883, one Matthew Cooney was brought before a special inquiry at Edenderry accused of stealing guns from Charles Colley Palmer of Rahan House.[127]

The minutes of the Poor Law Union meetings, usually held on Saturday at the workhouse, show that issues and debates at the meetings were often determined along party lines. Members were often put forward to promote party interests, as was Bernard Ennis, the Rhode 'Suspect' in 1881. Ennis was proposed by the parish priest and defeated the landlord David Kerr by twenty-eight votes to seven. The Conservatives had declared that the 1881 elections had been a 'marked defeat' for the Land League at Edenderry, but Ennis's success in the Ballyburley and Monasteroris division provided hope for the future.[128] The boardroom of the Poor Law Union at Edenderry offered the Home Rulers an opportunity to exert themselves and gain experience in public affairs, the first time that they could do such a thing. They also used it as an opportunity to face down the Conservatives, or who Charles Jellico referred to as 'the Orange clique'. When debating issues such as provisions for the workhouse and maintenance of the building, the voting was always divided between the Unionists and the Home Rulers. After the elections of April 1881, John Wakely of Ballyburley House was elected chairman of the Board of Guardians for the twenty-first consecutive years, underlining the Protestant domination of local politics.[129] By 1900 and after, it was possible for Catholic men, such as Patrick Duggan of Highfield House, to hold the position of chairman. Problems existed with voting, such as occurred in 1881 when it was claimed that two of those who voted for David Kerr of Rathmoyle House were non-resident in the area and thus not entitled to vote.[130] The franchise for the entire county at the this time was little over 3,500 so the number of those who were actually entitled to vote in the Edenderry elections would have been quite small. The extension of the franchise in 1884 also proved a factor in the mobilisation of popular politics at Edenderry. The Protestant members of the Board of Guardians who voted *en bloc* with each other at union meetings included Jasper Joly, David Kerr, S.W. Hendy, William J.H. Tyrell, Garrett Tyrell, Edward Robinson, Downshire's agent Thomas R. Murray and John Ridgeway who kept the minutes at meetings. It must be noted however that some Protestants such as Dr Robert Saunderson of Bella Vista House and William Smith of Ballyhegan House in Carbury supported the Edenderry Home Rule club at this time.

Nationalism 1885-1890

The Home Rule club and National League branch at Edenderry were more than just political groups; they were adamant that social conditions at Edenderry should improve and that education was an essential requirement for all creeds and classes. In June 1883 Michael Costello proposed at the Home Rule meeting that there was a need to establish, 'a suitable town hall in the town of Edenderry, in which the patriotic young men of the town and neighbourhood could hold social and intellectual reunions such as concerts, lectures, etc. and in connection with which a library and reading room could be established'.[131] The following month the committee purchased a house which would be converted into a hall for such purposes.[132] Presiding at the chair of the Irish National League branch in the town, Patterson implemented a scheme of prize-giving to the children of labourers who performed well in the school exams.[133]

However, they continued to oppose the actions of the local landlords and the Unionists on the Poor Law Union board, who were opposed to any concessions being given to the tenantry and especially the Labourers' Act. In November 1883 there was considerable unrest at the Union meeting over the Labourers' Act, where the Conservative/Unionists won a vote of twenty-seven – fourteen against implementing the building of houses for labourers. Costello pointed out that the Tullamore Union had already built sixty-six cottages for the poor there. At this point Kerr told Costello that the ratepayers would be unhappy with him for proposing extra taxes on their backs, and that if the ratepayers voted Costello out they would be better off for doing so. After heated exchanges Costello replied 'that it would be convenient for you and your crew if they did'.[134]

The National League called on all voters to claim their vote depending on what their tenement was worth e.g. if it was worth more than £20 they had two votes. This system of voting ensured that the Protestant position was maintained, but it would soon begin to change, starting with an increase to the franchise, which was brought in 1884. The possibility that Home Rule would come into effect was debated and both the National League and Home Rule party met in November 1884 to discuss how they would prepare themselves for the day when they would be in parliament.[135] The validity of Michael Delaney to sit on the Union board after the upcoming election was also discussed and Costello told the meeting that Delaney 'was doing the dirty work of the Edenderry Orangemen and the Freemasons'.[136]

As the elections of 1885 and the proposed Home Rule bill was debated and studied in detail around the country, the Nationalists at Edenderry were preoccupied with local issues, such as the support they showed for John Cassidy and the 'Croghan eviction'. In August 1885, the plight of John Cassidy, his wife and five children who had been evicted eighteen months previously by Lady Howard Bury, were highlighted as both John and his wife received a month's sentence in Tullamore jail for refusing to pay rents.[137] As he had done on many occasions, Terence O'Kearney White of Edenderry defended the accused at the assizes in Philipstown, for which the Rhode branch of the National League tendered their thanks for his 'very efficient and able manner in which he defended the felonious attempt of ultra Orangeism to deprive the Nationalists of their rights to franchise'.[138] There was a great demonstration in September 1885 to welcome Cassidy and his family back to Rhode at which many from Edenderry were present.[139]

The issue of sectarianism was always evident in the actions of both sides in the Board of Guardians, and in 1886 the Nationalists were up in arms

Edenderry in 1885.

after Terence O'Kearney White had not been appointed solicitor for the workhouse.[140] The *Leinster Leader* continued its humorous take on the Tyrell brothers claiming that Parnell must be quaking in his boots to hear that they were in opposition to him.[141] After nearly twenty years in existence, the Home Rule club dissolved when the club met on the 3 January 1886. Presiding at the meeting, William Moran told those attending that the time had come to disband. The Home Rule Bill of 1886 failed to pass in the House of Commons as the Conservatives, aided by some Liberals (who had defected), objected to the bill on grounds that it threatened Protestant interests and indeed the unity of the country.

However the disbandment of the Home Rule club was only temporary, as the National League held a massive demonstration in January 1886, which included speeches from four MPs including Sir Thomas Esmonde and Dr Fox. The meeting held at Killane was presided over by Revd Kinsella who told the crowd that they were 'still under Castle rule'. All classes including farmers, shopkeepers, labourers and artisans attended the demonstration. The speakers, including the radical Fr Connolly of Edenderry, condemned the evil system of land grabbing and landlordism. Connolly told the crowd assembled that the Orange hoard were on the verge of bankruptcy and reminded them that boycotting 'was a game that two can play'. There were further calls that the landlords were 'shonneen's and henchmen' and the demonstration finished with Kinsella stating that 'Cork may have its Bence Jones, Kerry its Sam Hussey and Kildare its Cloncurry, but none could hold a candle to Jasper Robert Joly and his two bum bailiffs Billy and Garrett Tyrell'.[142]

The first meeting of the newly formed Edenderry branch of the Irish National League included on the committee: Revd J. Kinsella, Revd J. Connolly, George Patterson, Charles Jellico, Denis Sheil, John Reddy, Joseph Fox, Michael Costello, Michael Paul O'Brien, Patrick McGuinness, William Moran, Edward Pelin, J. Moore, J.E.H. Patterson, Richard Brophy, J.P.H. Patterson, T. O'Kearney White and Joseph O'Brien, Joseph Mulvin, Mick Delaney, Terence Groome, John Farrell, James Kane, John Mulraney, Patrick Kennedy junior, William Hanlon, Dr Boyan, George O'Brien and William O'Brien.[143]

The tensions in the boardroom of the Poor Law Union continued and the issue of the Edenderry Labourers dominated proceedings in much of 1886 and 1887. In February 1887 Sylvester Rait Kerr caused a stir among the Nationalists when he said that it was nonsense to be listening to the comforts of the labourers, and Garrett Tyrell weighed in with his comments that Union business should not be wasted on such issues. The *Leinster Leader* commented that, 'old goosey Joly had stated that if there was to be a discussion to postpone it'.[144] There was also considerable unrest at this time over the insult, which had been given to Revd Andrew Hume of Rhode 'by a clique of the Orange freemasons'. Presiding in the chair Bernard Ennis, one of the 1881 'suspects', claimed that it was the greatest honour bestowed on a Catholic to defend a priest against the 'Scotch and Cromwell's men'.[145] The reference to the Scotch and Cromwell's men were obvious references to Rait Kerr and Wakely who had originally settled in the area after having fought in the pay of Cromwell.

In 1887 the House of Commons passed a coercion bill to counteract the spread of Nationalist organisations and the issue, like so many before, divided the Board of Guardians at the workhouse. In April 1887 Charles Jellico proposed that the guardians should oppose the bill, which was met with opposition by Thomas L. Dames who led the Conservatives from the room and abandoned the meeting.[146] A massive demonstration was organised in the market square, where Revd Hume, Revd Connolly and Revd E. O'Leary of Balyna presided. Appealing to the crowd to oppose the bill Revd Kinsella stated that the act was called the Crime Act Bill, but he was at a loss to know who the criminals were. Furthermore Kinsella added that the bill gave full scope to the landlords to put people off the land and replace them with emergency men. The meeting finished without any interruption from the RIC and the gathering was told that they would in time turn out 'Balfour and the rest of the gagging government'.[147]

The Nationalists of Edenderry throughout the 1880s adopted the tactic of boycotting against anyone who was found to be in league with the Unionists and emergency men. In May 1887 the National League in Edenderry proposed, 'that having heard that some of the traders calling themselves Nationalists are sending out their goods on objectionable cars, we call on all the members of this branch to see that no one who violates the rules of our organisation remains a member thereof'. They also called on all members where possible to promote the development of Irish industries. When this failed to deter those guilty of such offences, Kinsella decided to use the pulpit to call on all those 'who supply objectionable cars and bread to discontinue and we endeavour to stamp out land grabbing and grass grabbing of evicted farms'.[148]

As dedicated as the Nationalists were to the cause of Home Rule, many were reprimanded in 1887 for their failure to attend Union board meetings when important issues were being discussed. At the National League meeting in August, George Patterson reprimanded those who had failed to attend saying:

> … on many recent occasions when matters of importance were to be considered in the union boardroom, and the duly printed cards containing the usual information to tell the guardians that the matters to be considered were sent to them. And we hereby record our condemnation of these absentees' conduct, and that copies of this resolution be sent to the surrounding branches of the union.[149]

The *Leader* commented that the patriotic spirit of Edenderry had subsided and that during the days of the Land League it was 'red hot' and that now some members of the board don't bother going to the meetings. The consequence of the failure of some of the members not turning up was that Ridgeway and the Tyrell brothers had blocked the Labourers' Act.[150]

The Parnell Split – 'Politics from the pulpit'

The great achievement of Charles Stewart Parnell was that he had managed to put the issue of Home Rule on the agenda of English politics, and having successfully overcome the forged 'Piggott' letters and a libel claim against *The Times* newspaper, his career, it seemed in 1890, was clearly

Grange Castle, residence of the Tyrrell bothers.

in the ascendancy. However all that was to change when, in November 1890, his name was implicated in a divorce case involving his long-term partner Katherine O'Shea. Gladstone would not tolerate it and asked that he resign; this only a few months after receiving a standing ovation in the House of Commons. Opinion was divided, but the Catholic Church was staunchly opposed to him remaining in power. The Home Rule party and Nationalists at Edenderry were also divided over the issue and either stayed loyal and were known as Parnellites or opposed him and sided with the McCarthyites.[151]

Two of Edenderry's most influential Nationalists found themselves on opposite sides and launched scathing attacks on each other from whatever platform was available. The work that had been achieved in the previous decade and more in reviving a national interest at Edenderry was now divided. The Revd John Kinsella PP of Edenderry was anti-Parnell and resigned his position of chairman of the Edenderry branch of the National League, which was taken by George Patterson in January 1891. The National League meeting on 4 January had resolved: 'having regard to Charles Stewart Parnell's past political services to Ireland and his unrivalled political sagacity and wisdom, we consider him the only capable parliamentary leader of the

Edenderry Market House.

people of Ireland in obtaining their legislative independence'.[152] Kinsella refused to pass such a resolution and so was asked to step aside. There was a vote when Kinsella left the room and only Michael Costello of Ardbash House was against the resolution, while Hackett, Moran and Fox declined to vote. The split had been evident as the annual collection for party funds had been retained 'until we decide what to do with it'.[153]

The local branch of the National League was anxious to get Parnell to visit the town on his national campaign to seek support to remain in power. In Kinsella they had a sworn enemy of Parnell, and he frequently used the pulpit to castigate Parnell and appeal to the Nationalists at Edenderry to follow the McCarthyites. The *Leinster Leader* quipped that after Kinsella appealed to parishioners at a Sunday mass in February 1891 to wait after mass had finished to form a new branch, only four men remained: two ex-policemen and one the man in charge of the canal boat. The *Leader's* correspondent maintained sarcastically that it was a worthy beginning.[154] The departure of Fr Connolly from the parish in the summer of 1890 meant that Patterson and company had lost a firm supporter of Parnell and one who would have influenced Kinsella. At his farewell banquet in July 1890, Connolly had been described as 'a stern supporter of the rights of the weaker and humbler classes and a man who had proved himself a terror of the Orange ascendancy of this district'.[155] The Parnellites used the Poor Law Union meetings to propose support for Parnell as 'the trusted leader of the Irish race' and according to Charles Jellico they would resist any attempt to remove him 'at the dictation of an English statesman'.[156] The chairman of the Poor Law Union, John Ridgeway, would not accept the resolution and

The bending shop at Aylesbury's Mills.

argued that it would become a political debating society if he allowed it to pass. The Nationalists compared Ridgeway to Hamlet quoting the famous lines from the play 'Conscience does make cowards of us all', and said that he was fearful of how he and his fellow Unionists would be treated if Home Rule came into effect.[157]

At times the divide over the issue of Parnell became bitter and the Unionists looked on, happy that their interests would be secure as long as the Nationalists remained divided and at war with each other. The Revd Kinsella stated that on his side were 'the men of intelligence' and that their members were true to the principles of 'truth, justice and morality'.[158] Angered by Kinsella's public letter Patterson hit back at the McCarthyites and claimed that the men he represented did 'not strive to go without God' and stated that if support for Parnell made him 'obscure' he was proud to call himself one of the obscure few.[159]

The elections for the Poor Law Union were fought in 1891 among Parnellite/ McCarthyite platforms much to the pleasure of the Unionists. The poor showing in these elections, which saw men such as Charles Jellico refusing to stand, quickly altered Kinsella's stance and he appealed to the

John Wakely of Ballyburley House, *c.*1918.

Parnellites for the money that his branch were owed from party collections over the previous few years. Asking the branch to follow the way of God, he concluded, 'I am confident we will all be of one mind and one heart again.'[160] The National League's secretary Charles Jellico ordered that all funds were to stay in the possession of the Parnellites for the time being. On 6 October 1891 at Brighton in England, Charles Stewart Parnell died at only forty-five years of age. Attending his funeral at Glasnevin Cemetery on 11 October were, among others, Michael Costello, Charles Jellico and George Patterson who, despite having being advised by his doctor to not attend, mourned for Parnell in the heavy autumn rain. Twelve days later Patterson followed Parnell to his grave, having not recovered from illness. The Nationalists of Ireland had lost its leader, and Edenderry had lost its inspiration.

The bitter divide that existed over the Parnell spilt was evident in the fact that Revd Kinsella did not officiate at Patterson's funeral, which instead was carried out by Fr P. Bolger CC of Edenderry. That George Patterson had a great standing in the community and had the admiration of his adversaries, was seen in the fact that Thomas Murray and Charles H. Manners were among the mourners and John Wakely sent a wreath.[161] The *Leinster Leader* also commented on the esteem in which Patterson was held, in that Mr Aylesbury requested to make the casket (which he duly did, and which was said to be a magnificent one at that). The Aylesburys were Quakers and from Bristol, an example that the Whigs of Edenderry could never keep down Patterson.

Literary nationalism and pastimes

The magic of the quill

Another aspect of the Home Rule movement at Edenderry down through the years was the use of Nationalist literature to promote the cause of Ireland. There were many proponents of literary items published in the local newspapers including Patrick O'Kennedy, John O'Brien and later Seamus Haughton better known as 'Seamus from Clonmore'. The most important of these writers, however, was a man named Hugh Farrell, who was master of the workhouse. Much of what is known about Hugh Farrell is taken from Patrick O'Kennedy's 'Edenderry Scrapbook', which appeared in 1934 in the *Leinster Leader*. According to O'Kennedy he treated the subjects of his poetry with scorn and opposed the tyrants, mainly the landlords, who were the target of his dislike. In his book, *Carbury GAA*, John Cummins states that Hugh Farrell was a Dublin man who came to Edenderry as a teacher and was also working in the poorhouse at the turn of the century. However the 1901 census states that Farrell was born in King's County and that his wife Kate was from County Westmeath. Other information on his character suggests that he was the last person to be evicted locally from a smallholding in Codd near the Derries, and after this Revd Kinsella got him a job in the workhouse. Whatever his character or origins, he created quite a stir with his writings.

In 1873 he published a book entitled *Irish National Poems* under the name Aedh, which is Irish for Hugh. Many of the poems that he wrote, which were published in local newspapers, were done so using a pseudonym, the most frequent of which was 'PV Maro from Brindisi'. Dr Philip Brady details some of the poems that Farrell wrote, including the correspondence and reply to Frank Cronin's poem 'Farewell to Edenderry' in his book *A Place in Poetry*.[162] In his poem 'Farewell to the Sergeant', Farrell pokes fun at the RIC sergeant who had been transferred from Edenderry, claiming that Cronin's greatest success was keeping the streets of Edenderry free from stray dogs.[163]

In January 1893 Farrell was forced to retire from the workhouse on grounds of ill health and the issue of remuneration to him was debated for several weeks at the board meetings, where the Unionists members refused to pay him the proposed settlement. Obviously his Nationalist writings were something that angered the Unionist members of the board. At a meeting in February it was decided to give him a payment for his twenty-four years service but no extra of ten years as Charles Jellico had previously proposed.[164] He was replaced by Alexander Ralph Dagg who was appointed master of the workhouse on a salary of £50. Following his retirement he was involved with both Cronin and other unknown persons using the pseudonyms 'Venus' and 'Katie', in making jibes at each other through the medium of poetry which was published in the *Leinster Leader*.

Another writer and poet from Edenderry of this period used the pseudonym 'A.J.S.' and frequently wrote in the local newspapers about both local and national issues, which included the death of Parnell in 1891. In the memoriam to Parnell, 'A.J.S' lamented:

> All, all is over is o'er we've laid him down to rest,
> Amid a nation's mighty burst of grief,
> Tonight the clay lies heavy on the cold, cold breast of Ireland's honoured chief.

Another local poet named John O'Brien had poetry published in the English magazine *The Muses* including the poem 'The Poet' for which he was awarded a silver medal.

The poetry of both Padraig O'Kennedy and 'Seamus from Clonmore' was quite influential in this period and indeed well into the 1920s and '30s. At the turn of the century many people would have been familiar with the works of O'Kennedy who wrote frequently in the *Freeman's Journal*, the biggest selling newspaper of the day, and in the *Irish Weekly Independent*. His poems include 'Day dreams'[165], 'Paddy Dermody and the Leprechauns'[166] and 'The Legend of Croghan Hill'[167]. In his tribute to the Edenderry shops, which appeared in the *Leinster Leader* on 23 December 1905, O'Kennedy, through

Kinsella's Medical
Hall *c.*1915.

his lyrical verse, provides us with a picture of Edenderry at Christmas time
that year. Recalling the shops of the town, O'Kennedy states:

> Delaney's, Fay's, O'Toole's, O'Brien's,
> Miss Barber's toy shop and Miss Ryan's,
> The Railway House and Potterton's,
> Pat Moore's, Mike Byrne's and Miss Dunne's
> Are all mixed up in such a way
> Upon my notes I cannot say
> What Moore is selling, Hanlon, Fay,
> Or what the 'U.P.S.' display.

In 1934 O'Kennedy wrote in his 'Edenderry Scrapbook' more information
on the poet 'P.V. Maro from Brindisi' who had been involved with Constable
Frank Cronin in 1893 making jibes at each other in public correspondence.
At the bottom of the scrapbook O'Kennedy observed the following lines
signed Li Lo Pekin and dated 12 July 1923. The lines included:

> 'We searched for him far we searched from he near,
> Where was PV Maro?
> We found him at last, full of stout and beer, in thingummy's public house o!

> A bottle of anger, a pen of spite, before this 'near yet far' gent,
> Who scrambled away with a fierce delight
> His own farewell to the sergeant.

> He came not from any Italian vale, and never saw the Tiber,
> He did two years hard in Tullamore jail, picking oatlum into fibre.

Padraig O' Kennedy on
his wedding day.

O sergeant, o sergeant oh why have you gone,
From cleansing the streets and the bar o!
Your qui vive eye would have waved goodbye to mister Pee Vish Maro.

Sports and Leisure

Despite the obvious divide in society between Nationalists and Unionists,
Catholic and Protestant, sport and pastimes it seems transcended these
boundaries. Perhaps Edenderry is unique in this distinction, in that they
all enjoyed each other's company on the playing fields of various sports.
The GAA had been founded by Michael Cusack in 1884 and according
to him it 'had spread like wildfire through the country'. This fire it seems
took longer to reach Edenderry, for there was no GAA club founded in the

Edenderry
Cricket Team
in 1886.

town until 1891. The *Midland Tribune* commented in 1889 'the Edenderry
Cricket club will soon be in operation again this season. How is it that we
are so backward in this town regarding such sports as football and hurling
in this thriving town of 2,000 population'.[168] Prominent Nationalists such
as the Pattersons, O'Kearney Whites and the Murphy brothers, Tom and
John, were all keen members of the cricket team, despite the GAA's ban on
foreign games. There were as many as four cricket teams in the town at this
time namely Edenderry, Cloncannon, a team from M.P. O'Brien's U.P.S.
and from Aylesbury's. A typical team sheet that survives from this period,
lists the names of those who represented Edenderry on 23 August 1890
in a cricket match against Kilbeggan, in which Bannon and Traynor were
best for Edenderry. The team on that day included T. Harte, P. Gowran, E.
Traynor, T. Fulton, P. Bannon, T. Connell, W. Traynor, W. Foley, T. Foley, C.
Traynor and P. Swords.

Tennis was another popular pastime for the people of the town during
the period of Home Rule, but it was a centre of controversy in the summer of 1887. In April 1887 Thomas R. Murray, agent for Lord Downshire,
asked the tennis club to give up its grounds, which were situated on the Fair
Green. The tennis club had as its members some of those who refused to
pay the tolls at the market house in 1881, and this was seen as Murray's way
of gaining revenge. Mr James Galloghy, manager of the Ulster Bank, had
formed the club some years previously.[169] Cycling was another popular past
time in Edenderry; the Williams brothers Arthur and C.C. were prominent
members of the cycling club.

A report in the *Midland Tribune* in August 1895 noted that an 'enormous

C.C. Williams, Edenderry Cycling Club *c.*1890.

assemblage of the town and country folk thronged the Coneyboro road on last Friday evening' to watch a sixteen mile road race, and that racing had proved very popular in the locality, 'not even excepting the fairer sex, amongst whom are many ardent cyclists'. On this occasion the event was won by J. Malone closely followed by Slevin and Arthur Williams.[170]

The Unionists, as well as playing cricket alongside the Nationalists at Edenderry, also enjoyed their own leisure pursuits in the wintertime in the form of fox-hunting, and there was a district harriers' club known as the Edenderry Harriers. However one important Nationalist, Terence O'Kearney White, was amongst its members and frequently rode the track from 'Furry Hill' at Carbury to the home of Thomas Dames at Greenhills near Rhode. One such meet in 1896 included amongst its riders Charles Manners, Humphrey Bor, Dr Lancaster, Miss Russell, Miss Mahon, Mr Gasteen and Mr Hope.[171] Another meet assembled at Newberry Hall in 1903 included Mrs T. O'Kearney White, C.H. Manners and District Inspector Irvine of the RIC at Edenderry. The gentry around Edenderry also provided annual 'shoots' for guests at their estates, that of E.J. Beaumont Nesbitt's at Tubberdaly amongst the most popular. In 1986, Christopher Jones recalled how he had begun to work for Nesbitt in 1912 at 9s per week, and regularly worked during the hunts of grouse, rabbit and pheasant. An example of life in the 'big house' can be seen from Jones' account, in which he recalls working as a 'beater' at the hunt and being 'supplied with hampers of sandwiches, large pots of tea, while the visitors would be entertained in the mansion and accommodation provided for the night'. The valets would clean the guns and store them in a special room for the next day's hunting, which usually

Arthur Williams of the Edenderry Cycling Club *c.*1890.

lasted for three days. In 1921 Jones played a major role in the burning of Tubberdaly House during the War of Independence, which was to force the Beaumont Nesbitts from the area.[172]

Edenderry emigrants 1820-1920

Throughout the period 1820-1920 numerous people left Edenderry for various reasons and emigrated to the 'New World' and a new way of life. Some were forced to leave because of poverty and eviction from the land, some left to pursue religious vocations and others for adventure. While it is not possible to show an exact figure of the numbers that emigrated from the Downshire Estate, some of those who did emigrate left their mark in other parts of the world, and so their deeds can be recorded here. These include:

Thomas McCabe
In June 1893 Thomas McCabe wrote from Washington DC to the editor of the *Leinster Leader* outlining his memories of his old school friend George Patterson, whom he had only learnt had died. McCabe wrote how he remembered Patterson's 'brave, open and manly face, docile as a child, yet brave as a lion'. Recalling his schooldays with Patterson he mentions other school friends: the Furys, O'Briens, 'his chum' Egan, McNamaras, Berminghams, Keons, Delaneys, Ennis, Byrne, Dunne and Johnny Neary of Blundell Street.

Edenderry Harriers' hunt,
c.1903, at Newberry Hall.

He was born in 1830 and in October 1859 he left Edenderry and spent two years in New Orleans before leaving in February 1861 with Tom Hyland and Laurence Nolan, (an uncle of George Patterson's) – both natives of Edenderry. When the American Civil War broke out in 1861 the three men joined the Missouri Volunteers. Their captain was General Sheridan and under his command they fought gallantly at the Battle of Perryville Kentucky in 1862. McCabe recalled how wrestling matches were often contested between the men from King's County and Kildare when there was a stalemate in the war. At the time of his writing, McCabe was working in the US War and Navy Department under the Secretary for War, Daniel Lamont. He finished his letter by wishing all in Edenderry luck and expressing his hope that Home Rule would soon pass into law. The *Leinster Leader* in December 1917 reported the death of McCabe aged eighty-seven in Washington. The obituary recalled that the Hedge School Master Neddy Elliot had taught him in Edenderry. He had contributed frequently to the building of the new church in Edenderry and was in constant contact with Fr Murphy. In his latter years he was also a noted writer and contributed frequently to American literary journals.

Jack McComb
The following information is taken from the *Midland Tribune* 5 July 1902 which reported the death of Jack McComb under the heading 'Brave Edenderry man drowned while rescuing priest'. Quoting from the American newspaper the *Durango Democrat*, the *Tribune* gives an account of the death of Mr John McComb, a native of Edenderry, at Silverton, Colorado.

A Father O'Rourke was thrown by his horse over a precipice, into the turbulent waters of a river near Silverton. 'Jack' McComb, as he is familiarly referred to, jumped heroically to the rescue. The *Democrat* writes:

> Just as he was reaching for Father O'Rourke on the brink of the precipice, a
> rolling rock struck him on the head, knocking him into the stream, in an uncon-
> scious condition, as he was scarcely seen after going over the precipice. Father
> O'Rourke was also drowned. McComb passed under the bridge, and his body
> was located some distance below, by the rescuing party. There were two cuts on
> his head, one leg broken, and his clothes almost washed from his body. John
> McComb, or 'Jack' was widely known, as he had mined in all parts of Colorado
> but made his money in Leadville. He was one of the most generous and genial of
> men, a loyal friend, and a candid open foe; he was interested in mining in San Juan
> County, and reported to be en route to close a deal for the Galty Boy, when death
> overtook him. His home was in Denver, where his wife and daughter reside.

William J. Kelly, Jnr

For thirty years William Kelly, Jnr, was identified with newspaper work, and
during his residence of a quarter of a century in Kansas City, he became
widely known as circulator of the *Kansas City Star*, which was one of the
leading journals of the United States. He was a son of William Kelly, Snr, and
was born August 30 1862, in Albany, New York. A native of Ireland, William
Kelly, Snr, was born in Edenderry, King's County, in 1836. At the age of
seventeen he emigrated to the United States, landing in New York City. He
was a leather inspector in Albany for some time, after which he was for a
while engaged in agricultural pursuits in Franklin County, Kansas. Going
next to Kansas City, Missouri, he was employed in the freight department of
the Missouri Pacific Railroad Company until his death in March 1898. He
was a member of the Baptist Church and belonged to Triple Link Lodge,
No. 9, Independent Order of Odd Fellows, of Kansas City, Missouri. He
married Elizabeth White, who was born in Navan, County Meath.

Brought up in Albany, New York, William Kelly, Jnr, was educated in the
schools of that city. Accompanying his parents to Ottawa, Kansas, in 1879, he
remained on the home farm for two years, assisting in its labours. Mr Kelly
moved to Kansas City, Kansas, in the autumn of 1886 for the purpose of
becoming agent and circulator of the *Kansas City Star*. With the growth of
the city, and under the efficient management of its circulators, Mr Kelly and
his brother, George H. Kelly (who had charge of the Kansas City, Missouri
territory), the circulation of the paper has rapidly increased, twenty-three
thousand copies being now daily distributed in Kansas City. Kelly was

Typical market-day scene at
Edenderry *c.*1910.

always active in all movements for the betterment of civic conditions in his
hometown and was a member of the Mercantile Club, having been a direc-
tor for a longer time than any other member. He served the organisation as
first vice-president and chairman of important committees. He was president for three years of the Associated Charities and was a member of Tau
Ro Mee, No. 30, of the Ancient Order of United Workmen. He took a leading part in the law enforcement movement that made Wyandotte County a
law-abiding community.[173]

Bishop John Rooney

John Rooney was born in Edenderry on 26 January 1844 and, having
entered into the priesthood, was transferred to the Cape of Good Hope
in South Africa. It was here on 29 January 1886 that he was appointed
Coadjutor Vicar Apostolic of the Cape of Good Hope, Western district, as
well as being Bishop of Sergiopolis. He was succeeded from this position
in 1908, and retired from the priesthood in 1925. Two years later on 27
February he died and was buried in Capo di Buona Speranza.

Peter F. Kelly

Born in Edenderry in 1848, he was initially a member of the Royal Irish
Constabulary, and at the age of twenty-three went to the United States. He
settled in New York City and was employed with Thurber & Co., where he
remained as a trusted employee for many years. In 1885 he went to Brooklyn,
and became involved with the liquor business at the corner of Court Street
and Hamilton Avenue. Kelly was a member of Court Thomas Francis Meagher,
Friends of America, and was vice-president of the Liquor Dealers' Association
of the Forty-fifth District. He was interred in Calvary Cemetery in April 1906.

The Canal Harbour *c.*1900.

Michael Flanagan

The following information about Michael Flanagan is taken from the *Midland Tribune*, 13 February 1904 in an article entitled 'Windfall for Edenderry Man':

> Patrick Flanagan from near Edenderry has recently been declared by the Supreme Court of Pennsylvania to be the sole next of kin to a man named Michael Flanagan, who died in Pittsburgh in 1899. Flanagan arrived in America at the age of ten in 1847 and was employed by a Pittsburgh blacksmith by the name of Ashe of whose business he afterwards became foreman. Later on he started business on his own behalf and at the time of his death his fortune was said to be in the region of $70,000.
>
> Several claimants immediately staked their claim to his fortune but as a result of personal investigations made by a Commissioner of the American Courts, Patrick Flanagan has been named as the sole next of kin. Mr T. O' K. White, solicitor, Edenderry, acted for Flanagan.

Cornelius Heeney

A merchant and philanthropist, Cornelius Heeney was born in Edenderry in 1754 and died in Brooklyn, USA, 3 May 1848. After working in the brewery of Robert Fullard in Edenderry (Fullard died in 1797 and subsequently his wife and three children emigrated to the USA), Heeney emigrated to America in 1784 and became a fellow employee of the founder of the Astor family in the store of a New York fur dealer. His employer, retiring, left the business between John Jacob Astor and Heeney, and they prospered in it for several years and then separated. Heeney continued in the same line and amassed a considerable fortune.

He was a bachelor and used his income in the promotion of religious and charitable works; St Peter's church, St Patrick's and the Catholic Orphan Asylum, New York, were recipients of generous gifts. He was one of the first Catholics to hold public office in New York, and served five terms in the State Assembly from 1818 to 1822. He retired from business in 1837 and went to live in Brooklyn, where he had purchased a large farm. Here, he continued his charitable benefactions, and having spent the most of his income for so long in good works, he planned to secure the disposition of the whole of his estate for the same purpose. Accordingly it was incorporated by Act of Legislature, 10 May 1845, as 'The Trustees and Associates of the Brooklyn Benevolent Society' with the object of administering the estate for the benefit of the poor and the orphans.

Most Reverend Andrew Killian

Andrew Killian was born on 26 October 1872 at Edenderry, the son of Nicholas Killian and his wife Eliza Josephine, *née* Ryan, who were schoolteachers. His grandfather Nicholas Killian had conducted a 'hedge school' during the Penal Laws of the eighteenth century. Andrew was educated at Mungret Jesuit College, Limerick, and St Patrick's College, Carlow. He graduated with a B.A. from the Royal University of Ireland in 1894, and was ordained a priest on 4 June 1898. He went to Australia later that year where his younger brother Patrick and sister Mary were also working in the Australian Catholic Church.

Killian's first appointment was as an assistant priest in the parish of Bourke in western New South Wales. In 1907 he visited Ireland and the following year he was transferred to Broken Hill. He subsequently filled the offices of parish priest; administrator of the cathedral; dean, and vicar-general (1919). In 1919 he was designated a domestic prelate of the Holy See. He cleared the parish of debt, extended the bishop's house and built St John's School at Broken Hill North. Elected bishop of the neighbouring South Australian diocese of Port Augusta, he was consecrated on 15 June 1924 in the pro-cathedral at Peterborough. Between 1924 and 1933 the bishop travelled thousands of miles visiting the scattered parishes of his vast diocese, which stretched from the eastern to the western border of South Australia. In 1926 he attended the Eucharistic Congress at Chicago; on this journey he was received by the Pope in Rome and visited Ireland again. In July 1933 Killian was appointed coadjutor archbishop of Adelaide to assist the ailing Archbishop Spence. When Dr Spence died the following year, Killian became archbishop.

Bishop Andrew Killian.

Despite the Depression, it was an era of expansion for the church. Archbishop Killian cited as the achievements of which he was proudest: the reopening of the historic school at Penola, originally founded by Mother Mary McKillop; the opening of the juniorate of the Sisters of St Joseph at Cowandilla; the arrival of the Carmelite Sisters in the diocese, and the National Catholic Education Congress of 1936.

He is most remembered for the congress. The first such gathering in Australia, it was arranged to mark the State's centenary. In announcing the event the archbishop said, 'The Education Congress will enable us to consolidate our forces behind the movement and enable us to acquaint our fellow-citizens of the sacrifices made by us. Catholics should know and understand the sacrifices made for Catholic Education.' Papers were presented by leading Catholic educationists about the work of Catholic schools and the congress ended with a Eucharistic procession of 100,000 people through Adelaide's streets. He died on 28 June 1939 in the Mercy Hospital, East Melbourne, and was buried in West Terrace cemetery, Adelaide.[174]

Edenderry Town Council and the decline of Home Rule

With the failure of the second Home Rule bill in 1893, Nationalist politics, it seemed, declined in Edenderry. The business people, Unionists and Nationalist alike, feared that they would lose all value on their produce should Home Rule ever be introduced as Garrett Tyrell had warned in 1893.[175] A picture of what the town looked like at this period might be appropriate and it seemed that the fortunes of Edenderry were never better. *The King's County Directory* for 1890 describes Aylesbury's Mills as 'doing a large amount of business in steam bending, wheel-making, turning, chair-making etc, and gives a great deal of employment'. In 1894 *Slater's Directory* estimated that there were 'fifteen spirit dealers, six being grocers, one draper, a baker, four butchers, four car owners, two coachbuilders, two blacksmiths, two tailors, two watchmakers, two insurance agents, two banks and three boot makers, one of which was a leather seller as well'. There were sixty-eight commercial undertakings in the town; surgeons and solicitors were considered to be professional people.

However the plight of the poor and the working classes at Edenderry at the century's end portrays a different picture of life in the town at this time. For many the workhouse was the only option and in 1895 the number of inmates residing there was never below 100. The conditions of those working in the workhouse in 1900 were recorded when it was claimed that the nurse 'sometimes is half suffocated by a smokey chimney and in the rainy season the use of an umbrella in her apartment is almost indispensable'. The report further claimed that her fortunes are vastly different from that of a nurse in England whose only concern 'was to have a sea view'.[176] In March

Jim Byrne's forge.

1900 John Kenny of the Edenderry Trade and Labour League wrote to the Edenderry No.1 Rural District Council complaining about the unsanitary conditions of the houses in the town. According to Kenny it was 'scandalous the way the different sexes are huddled together in one room' and that in some houses 'five families of more than ten people live under the one roof'.[177] A report in the *Westmeath Nationalist* in May 1896 highlighted the plight of the residents of the town, who were now exposed to an epidemic of scarlet fever. The guardians of the workhouse, it was claimed, looked on 'as the Council of Florence looked on the Great Plague until it was too late'.[178] This is in contrast to a report in 1891, which praised the 'friendly and fatherly' figure, Thomas R. Murray, because the streets of Edenderry were the model of cleanliness.[179] The Board of Guardians provided for some relief to the poor in 1898 when thirty-eight cottages were built in the town costing just under £6,000.[180]

Two events occurred in Edenderry towards the end of the nineteenth century, which rekindled the Nationalist spirit of the people of the town. The centenary celebrations of the 1798 Rebellion were performed in great style. With the hope that Home Rule or some form of self-government would someday become law, the Nationalists of Edenderry formed a '98 club called the Fr Kearns/Col Perry branch and set about organising the centenary celebrations. Its members included Patrick O'Brien, William Kennedy and Patrick Barry who formed a brass band which played at all the local celebrations that year including a great public demonstration in Rhode in April 1898 and on Carbury Hill in May. A most impressive demonstration was held in Monasteroris graveyard in July where William Kennedy told the crowd that Kearns and Perry were 'as true martyrs to liberty as ever breathed'.

Padraig O' Kennedy.

A huge Celtic cross had in 1874 been erected over the graves of the Wexford rebels. A grand nephew of Moses Kearns from County Wexford was present and asked the congregation to 'advance the sacred cause of Ireland' and to always honour the memory of Kearns and Perry.

The revival was also spearheaded by those like Padraig O'Kennedy who frequently gave lectures on the importance of Irish history, love of country and the native language. The formation of a branch of the newly formed United Irish League, which helped heal the split over Parnell in 1890, was formed in Edenderry in 1899. The branch gave itself the name the 'Edenderry Wolfe Tone United Irish League' and following its meeting on Saturday nights, would listen to a lecture from O'Kennedy.[181] The Manchester Martyrs were also remembered at Edenderry when in December 1899 an 'imposing display' was organised by the Working Men's Club, in which in open defiance of the RIC, Irish, French and Transvaal flags were waved, as well as loud cheers for the Boers. This was despite the fact that men from the town had gone to fight in the British Army in the Transvaal against the Boers. These included James Murray, Private Gowran, T. Stapleton and George Grey. Earlier in the year, a demonstration in August was reported to have been attended by 1,000 people, many on horseback, where the French *tricolore* was waved.[182]

The success of the United Irish League was short-lived however, despite the fact that John Kelly was on the Central Executive of the league for

King's County.[183] In 1900 Mr Haviland Burke, MP for King's County, visited Edenderry on a number of occasions in an effort to revive the interests
of the League but to no avail. He commented that it was a sad state of affairs
for Edenderry, as in the years previous they had always been a patriotic band
of brothers. In September 1901 those attending mass were chastised about
the poor support the United Irish League was receiving by Revd Kinsella,
who stressed that among the aims of the UIL were; to 'relieve the condition
of the hard working classes of Ireland and stemming the tide of emigration',
which he believed was leaving the country weaker and weaker each year.[184]

The Gaelic League branch at Edenderry was also struggling at this period
and the members complained that it was not getting the support of the
people of the town to promote its patriotic aim. In March 1900 the Gaelic
League could not find a delegate to go to the National Convention in
Dublin and the *Leader* asked, 'Is it the case that only fifteen people care
about the Irish language in Edenderry?' The classes of the Gaelic League
were held twice weekly in the Old Boys School on Wednesday and Sunday.
Matters were not helped when D.P. Moran, a teacher in the school, resigned
as the League's secretary in December 1900 for personal reasons. He had
been the League's chief promoter in the area.

In March 1900, Thomas R. Murray of Blundell House sold to Cambridge
University the collection of Irish antiquities, which had been found during
the previous seventy years at Edenderry. The collection had been stored
in the museum at the Town Hall and included items found at Ballykilleen
Hill from the Iron Age and items found in the River Boyne at Kishawanna.
The items included had been found when excavations were carried out in
1851 at Kishawanna Bridge, 1854 at William Morris's farm at Drumcooley
and in 1859 on Drumcooley Hill. Murray (who had been replaced by a Mr
McClintock in 1893 as agent of the Downshire estate), accepted £150 for
the collection on the condition that it would be forever kept separate from
the other collections in the museum of General Archaeology and Ethnology
and placed under the name the 'Murray Collection'. He also stated that the
sets of objects from separate digs shall never be broken up or divided. The
Cambridge Antiquary Society and other donors gave the money to finance
the venture.[185] Amongst the items from the Edenderry Museum, which are
now in Cambridge, include a 1798 pike; the sword of Tippo Sahib taken by
a man from Edenderry at the Battle of Seringapatam and given to Revd
James Colgan; a stone communion table from Monasteroris Franciscan
Abbey; and many Iron Age ornaments. A curious addition to the collec-

Moore's Butchers, Main
Street, 1919.

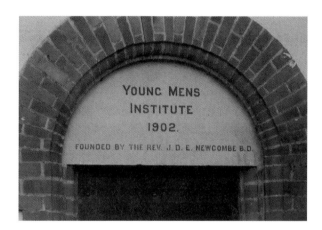

Young Men's Institute,
built in 1902.

tion was a marble slab which had been taken from Blundell Castle with
the inscription 'to the memory of Christian Forester and Prince Albert of
Brandenburg who came over in the year 1689'.

The Local Government Act of 1898 paved the way for the formation of
County Councils, which would run the affairs of the county. The act also
provided for district councils, one of the most successful of which was at
Edenderry. Prior to 1898 there had been Rural District Councils, which
incorporated the townlands around Edenderry and were overseen in the
main by those of the Union board. Following the elections of April 1899,
(the Nationalists at Edenderry receiving 365 votes (93.35 per cent) while
the Unionists received 26 votes or 6.65 per cent), the path was cleared for
local affairs to be decided by the people of the town.[186]

The Towns Improvement Act of 1854 allowed for 'town' status to be given

Train at Edenderry *c.*1900.

to those with a population of over 1,500 people. The 1891 census showed that Edenderry had a population of 1,577 people and so measures were put in place to apply for 'town' status. On 4 October 1902 the ratepayers gathered in the town hall to take legal steps to form such a body of Town Commissioners. The ratepayers signed the petition which was drawn up by Terence O'Kearney White and the names of twenty-one local government electors was also required if status was to be given. The Edenderry Town Commissioners came into being in February 1905 with nine commissioners approved for the town.

Prior to its inception the town had been criticised for its appearance, with basic things like lighting and footpaths of major concern. The *King's County Chronicle* commented in 1899 that 'after waiting for many long and weary years the inhabitants of Edenderry have at last awakened to the fact that pedestrians make their journeys through the streets at great disadvantages as there is no light to guide the weary traveller'.

The first chairman of the Town's Commissioners was M.P. O'Brien who held the position until he died in 1908. The law required that one third of the members of the council leave office each year after 16 January, which was the day of election. However a retiring officer could go forward for re-election and was usually unopposed. For the record, the first nine commissioners of Edenderry Town Council were: Michael P. O'Brien, Daniel Aylesbury, Michael Delaney, George Dunne, Dennis Fay, Patrick Moore, Patrick O' Brien, J.P.H. Patterson and John Pelin. The town clerk was Charles H. Manners. The council, upon its inception, was overwhelmingly Nationalist, which showed that the power of the landlord and of the Unionists was beginning to decline.

Michael Paul O'Brien, owner of
the UPS.

The first major reform was the lighting of the town, which was carried out
by M.P. O'Brien's gasworks company. The town council did not have the
power to borrow money and so the members pledged their own personal
security and borrowed £1,200 to finance the lighting of the town. At this
time they also carried out the resurfacing of the road from Monasteroris
to New Row corner, which was said to have been in a miserable condition. The Wyndam Land Act of 1903 brought about the break-up of many
of the landlord estates around Edenderry and measures were put in place
for the sale of land at the Downshire estate to the tenants living there. The
land act was part of the British Government's policy of 'killing Home Rule
with kindness'. Speaking in Edenderry in November, Haviland Burke MP
warned the tenants of the Downshire estate against buying their holding at
'fancy prices' indicating that hard times were ahead for many farmers.[187]

The Town Commissioners, it would seem, spent much of the early part
of the new century trying to deal with bringing about improvements in
the town, and so political issues took a back seat. An annual agricultural and
industrial show from 1905–1912 showcased much of what Edenderry had to
offer, another example of the hard work of the Town Commissioners.[188]

The *Leinster Leader* commented in 1909 that the main aim of the Town
Commissioners in Edenderry was to avoid media coverage and carry out
necessary work in the town. It further added that the 'promised scheme for
improving the footpaths remains only to be carried out to reflect honour
and credit on this little heard of and unassuming body'. It seems the scheme

Building the Girls'
National School, 1910.

The furniture loft at
Aylesbury's Mills.

was carried out by 1911, when the Commissioners were lauded for having 'materially helped the uprise of the town and earned for it the reputation it now enjoys'. Another factor for the success of the town council was the fact that they had never burdened the ratepayers for a penny towards the cost of these improvements.

It wasn't until 1915 that re-elections were contested although there were numerous changes in personnel on the council. These included William Corrigan, T.F. O'Toole, Arthur Williams, Andrew Byrne and Henry Patterson (who replaced M.P. O' Brien), George R. Dunne, Patrick O'Brien, Patrick Moore and J.H. Patterson. In 1915 outgoing officers John Pelin, Arthur Williams and Michael Delaney were opposed and they responded by issuing

Wheel made in Aylesbury's Mills.

handbills to the townspeople. The *Leader* paid tribute to the Commissioners, stating that:

> Members never sought publicity for their doings, and the good that they have achieved was never trumpeted beforehand, but 'grew' practically without anyone knowing it until the work was in progress. The limited taxation imposed has been well utilised, and if Edenderry boasts today of being up to date in its appearance and progress a goodly portion of the credit must be given to the little body which guides its administration.

The emergence of the Irish Volunteers, formed in November 1913 to counteract the threat of the Ulster Volunteers, briefly revived Nationalist politics at Edenderry. As a member of the Edenderry branch of the volunteers, Joseph Kelly recalled that 'all the able bodied men in the town seemed to be in the movement' but that the uniform meant more to them than the politics of the day. Recalling the uniform with pride, Kelly stated that they were so pleased with the 'black peaked volunteer caps and body belts of black leather and our Irish Volunteer badge'.[189] In September 1914, at a review of the Volunteers in Philipstown by Colonel Moore, 300 volunteers from Edenderry attended, many having travelled on canal boats. According to Kelly, this 'jaunt on the canal boats sounded the death knell of the local

Mansel Longworth Dames, died of pneumonia, 1909.

volunteers'. An incident occurred before the party reached Philipstown; the French flag having been raised caused uproar as, for many, it resembled too much its British counterpart and so it was soon replaced by a green flag with a harp.[190] Within days, John Redmond, leader of the Home Rule party, gave a speech which divided the Volunteer movement and many enlisted to fight in Europe beneath the 'Union Jack'.

Edenderry men in the 'Great War' 1914-18

The third and final Home Rule bill passed through the House of Commons on 11 April 1912, introduced by Prime Minister Asquith. The previous year, on 18 August, the Parliament Act enacted that the power of veto was restricted to two years and so Home Rule would pass into law in 1914.[191] An incident on the streets of Sarajevo heralded the outbreak of the First World War and so the issue of Home Rule was shelved until at least the war's end. The British Government maintained that the war would be over in a matter of months and after it, a new parliament would be set up in Dublin. The leader of the Irish Home Rule party, John Redmond, called on his followers to join the British Army and help their war effort. At Woodenbridge in County Wicklow in July 1914, Redmond called on the Irish Volunteers to fight 'as far as the firing line extends.'

The Irish Volunteers split after Redmond's speech over the issue of fighting for the British Army in the trenches of Europe. The estimated strength of the Army in July 1914 stood at 110,000, of which about 10,000 remained in the Irish Volunteers, the rest siding with Redmond. Many men from Edenderry went to fight for the British Army in the trenches of Europe; their bones now lie scattered across many European countries. The Unionist population, adversely opposed to any form of Home Rule, and who had formed themselves into armed groups in 1913 and 1914, saw the First World War as their chance to show their loyalty to the crown. Again the sons of the gentry and Protestants around Edenderry volunteered to fight for Britain but for reasons different to those of the Irish Volunteers.

Interestingly, some of the men from Edenderry that enlisted gave their

E.W. Mather killed in action in WWI.

nationality as 'British', as did Patrick Nestor, John Wright and James Carroll. James Carroll is actually buried in Monasteroris Graveyard, and is the only accounted soldier that was returned home to be buried. Most of the soldiers from Edenderry who had been members of the Irish Volunteers belonged to the Royal Dublin Fusiliers, although some, like Thomas Gill of New Row Corner, joined the Royal Irish Fusiliers. Sergeant Matthew Boyle, a former teacher in the Boys' National School under the Principal Edward Walsh, joined the Australian Army and was killed in action in France in January 1918. The sons of the Protestant gentry, however, enlisted in other units and would not serve alongside their Nationalist counterparts. Men such as Samuel Robinson joined the North Irish Horse regiment, while the Nesbitts of Tubberdaly and the Rait Kerrs of Rathmoyle House were made Lieutenants and Captains in English regiments owing to the social standing of their families. Details of some of those that enlisted show migration into Edenderry was occurring at this time; Cecil Quinn from Ballyshannon in County Donegal, Michael Dunford from County Kerry and Alex McBride from Omagh in County Tyrone (who had been a painter in Edenderry before the war) all enlisted in Edenderry. McBride died in 1919 from injuries sustained during the war and was interred in Monasteroris graveyard. He was married to a daughter of John Dunne of Main Street, Edenderry.

   Among the names of the men that volunteered from Edenderry and the surrounding areas were: Behan, Blong, Brennan, Broughall, Bryan, Carroll, Cassidy, Connell, Cronin, Cullen, Fulton, Gill, McCann, McGuinness,

WWI Medal given to
Private Nolan.

McNamee, Mulrein, Nelson, Quinn, Rait Kerr, Smith, Traynor, Walker and
Odlum. Many of these men were decorated for their bravery during the
war, including William Rait Kerr who was given the DSO medal, Bernard
Mulrein who received a Military medal, and John Sweeney who received
the '1914 Star'. The locations at which they fell are various, but men from
Edenderry fell at some of the better-known battles of the 'Great War'
e.g. Thomas Fulton at Mudros in Greece, George Nelson at the Somme,
Sylvester Rait Kerr at Ypres and Laurence Broughall at Gallipoli.

It would appear that many of the men who volunteered from Edenderry
and fought in the First World War were from families who had a connection
to the British Army in the past. Thomas Fulton was one of two brothers
who joined; ironically James was injured in the 1916 Rising in Dublin while
in a British uniform. Their uncle John Fulton had fought in the Boer War
and was injured at the Battle of Pietermaritzburg in South Africa in 1901.
Another family, whose plight during the First World War stands out, is that
of the Mulraneys of Carrick. In 1909 Christy died of malaria on his way to
India, after joining the army at eighteen years of age. Five years later Barney
was shot in France, while Bill was shot in Dublin during the 1916 Easter
Rising. The Mulraneys had been part of the first Gaelic football team in
Edenderry in the 1890s, known as the John Boyle O'Reilly's. Barney had
been a Sergeant in the 7th Bedford's division and is said to have fallen gallantly leading a charge of men.[192]

Employees at Aylesbury's
Mills.

The people of Edenderry were also quick to lend a hand to those who were suffering and displaced because of the war. A committee was formed to raise funds to take in Belgian refugees, and in late 1914 Mrs Nesbitt of Tubberdaly House took in a family of four. After several fundraising events in the town the sum of £37 was raised for the refugees of the war, while Aylesbury's Mills employed two Belgian workers in June 1915.[193] Despite the horrors of the war and the stalemate that existed in the trenches of Verdun and the Somme, recruitment remained constant at Edenderry. In March 1916 (when the IRB leadership had plans well in place for the Rising at Easter), T.R. Dixon, Recruiting Officer for the King's County, attended a meeting of the Edenderry Town Commissioners, which Denis Fay presided over as chairman. After hearing Dixon's request for more troops, they decided to form themselves into a committee to stimulate recruitment in that part of the King's County.[194]

The *Leinster Leader* reported the deaths of soldiers from Edenderry and frequently printed letters received by relatives back in Edenderry. One such letter received was from a Corporal William Glen who relayed the death of Private John Wright of Edenderry, a stretcher-bearer, to his family. Glen wrote:

John had been in my section since April last year, and was one of the oldest stretcher-bearers we had. I can assure you he was very much missed; he was such a good soldier. He was respected by all who knew him. We saw to his funeral and are looking after his grave. We had two beautiful crosses placed

Ballindoolin House.

on it, also some small crucifixes. Everything was done just as you would have wished.

The same edition of the *Leinster Leader* included a note from Private Joe Judge of Edenderry, writing to Wright's brother saying that, 'John lived about two hours and was buried in a very nice graveyard. The boys put a cross over his grave.'[195]

Grudgingly, the *Leader* also reported the exploits of Protestant men from Edenderry in the 'Great War', such as that of Dr Hamilton of Edenderry who was promoted to captaincy in January 1915. The DSO medal received by William Rait Kerr was also reported, as he led his men into battle at the Messines Ridge saying, 'It is better to die fighting than die running away. I will lead you. Charge.'[196] In July 1916 both Jack Connolly and Alex McBride received the parchment cert for gallant conduct and devotion to duty. Prior to enlisting in the army, both had been members of the Ancient Order of Hibernians, a Nationalist group in which McBride was an accomplished bandmaster. Connolly was described as being a mere boy and a native of the Tunnel, Edenderry.[197]

Despite the horrors and futility of all the fighting, some of the exchanges during the war are humorous, such as the story related to what happened at Suvla Bay, where some of the worst fighting of the war occurred. While landing at Suvla Bay, Thomas Fulton was beside Thomas Connor from Edenderry and they bade each other goodbye, as they both believed they would never see each other again. When the fighting had finished that day, the first person that Fulton met was Connor, who asked, 'You were not

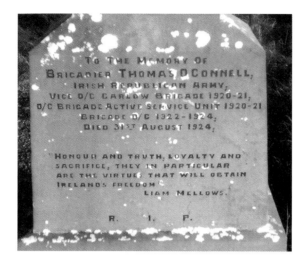

Vol. Thomas O'Connell's
headstone at Monasteroris.

killed?' To which Fulton replied, 'No, were you?'[198] Writing home to his
father at Ballindoolin House, William Upton Tyrell, who was wounded
at the Battle of the Somme on 1 July 1916, noted that he had recovered
and had taken a trip beyond enemy lines where he had 'shot some Huns'.
However, recalling the horrors of war, he wrote in June 1916 that 'this is the
wettest day that I have ever seen in this country and the place is a foot deep
in mud'. He survived this war and later fought in the Second World War
serving in India and the Far East.[199]

Many other casualties are reported in the newspapers of the day, which
illustrates the worry that some of the families had to endure while waiting
on news of their loved ones. In May 1917 Mrs Behan of New Row Corner
received word that her son Patrick (known as 'Parky') was dead, despite having been told some months previously that he might have been in a German
POW camp and still a prisoner.[200] Another mother awaiting news of her son
was Mrs Connell of New Row, whose son Patrick was killed at Cambrai
after the Germans captured a medical camp where he was been treated for
a wound.[201] It is ironic that Patrick Connell's brother, Thomas, was later
a member of the IRA. In a corner of a graveyard in the French town of
Cambrai, Patrick Connell now lies, buried in a British Army uniform; while
next to the graves of Kearns and Perry in Monasteroris, Volunteer Thomas
Connell lies buried, having fought to rid Ireland of British rule.

On 11 November when the war was officially declared over, many people
flew Union Jack flags on the Tunnel Road at Edenderry, which had been

given to many soldiers, some of whom had arrived home and were greeted through the town. That night Nationalist songs were sung, and ironically many used Republican colours in the parade through the town.[202] Over fifty years later, in 1970, a report in the *Leinster Leader* noted that at the Edenderry Branch of the British Legion the members passed their congratulations to John Webb and Patrick Mooney, veterans of the First World War, who had recently turned ninety years of age. In July 1918 the *Leader* had reported that Webb, along with Laurence Bell, had been injured in the war.

The independence struggle
at Edenderry 1916-21

In post Civil War Ireland a common taunt to those on opposing sides was to ask, 'Where were you at Easter Week?' As previously highlighted, the Edenderry Town Commissioners had only a month before the rebellion in Dublin actively sought to help stimulate recruitment for soldiers for the British war effort. In 1913 the RIC District Inspector had reported that most parts of King's County were relatively quiet, with the exception of Edenderry, where cattle-driving was resorted to from time to time. In March 1910, RIC intelligence in Edenderry reported that the Sinn Féin club had thirty members, but by 1915 it was virtually non-existent. How well-advanced militant nationalism was at Edenderry is hard to gauge, but what is certain is that Edenderry was represented in the fighting during Easter week in Dublin. Michael Foley who lived on the Main Street was interned in Frongoch in Wales in the aftermath of the 1916 Rebellion. The enigmatic Fr Paul Murphy had also come to the attention of the RIC who, in late 1916, reported that he was 'disloyal for a number of years' and that, together with other priest in the county, he was 'pro-German'.[203]

The Board of Guardians had by this time become overtly Nationalist with men such as Andrew Byrne and Denis Sheil prominent players in the boardroom. The board condemned the imprisonment of certain Irishmen in January 1916 and circulars were read and adopted by such figures as the O'Rahily and Joseph Plunkett. Following the Easter Rising, the Tullamore Town Council condemned the Rising and its chairman John Condron launched a stinging stack on the rebels. At the Offaly GAA County Board meeting, Edward Maloney of Edenderry, who was president of the Edenderry Hurling club, was appointed in Condron's place as delegate to the Leinster council, as the members of the board were opposed to Condron on his opinions of the 1916 Rising.

The people of Edenderry were very much occupied with the final settlement of the Downshire estate in 1916, a process which had begun in 1903 but which would still be undecided in the 1920s. In July 1916 there was a meeting of the tenants in the town hall to discuss certain proposals made by the Marquess of Downshire. At the meeting George O'Brien of Ballykillen presided and the people were informed of O'Kearney White's constant contact with the landlord's solicitors at Hillsborough. The people had signed the purchase agreements thirteen years previously but still the settlement was undecided. In twenty-three cases the full amount of purchase had not been given, and in a further thirty-five cases nothing had been paid at all. The land commission had offered a price of £4, 284 to the tenants to buy their land but there was a deficit of £876. The people were greatly angered by Downshire's refusal to sell the bogs. A committee was appointed to look into this matter and to further correspond with Hillsborough and the trustees appointed included Revd Murphy, Digby Odlum, Denis Sheil, G.O. Brien, John Foran, James Mooney and John Dempsey. Among those who still owed money to the Marquess of Downshire for a final settlement included John Farrell of the Derries; Michael Moore of Shean and Dora Whelan at Drumcooley. In the town itself, Katie Kennedy, Dora Manners, William Jackson, J. Corrigan, J.J. Barnes, Chris Donahue, Catherine Saunderson and James Whittaker.[204]

The construction of the new Catholic Church in the parish (by Fr Paul Murphy) occupied much of the time of the people of the town, as fundraising events of all kinds were undertaken to pay for the build. Open-air concerts, which included signing, dancing and storytelling, were commonplace. The workers of Aylesbury's Mills met in February 1917 at the Forrester's Hall to form themselves into a Trade Union to protect the workers' rights. They were addressed by Sean Tracey who represented the machinists in the mills, and a Mr Mulcahy, secretary of the National Trade Union of Ireland. By 1920 they had become more vocal and even prevented lorries leaving the mill with goods bound for many provincial towns.[205] The branch of the Irish National Forrester's at Edenderry known as the Fr Kearns branch, which had been formed in 1913, came under scrutiny in 1917 for a misappropriation of party funds. The motto of the Forrester's 'Unity, Nationality and Fraternity' it was claimed was non-existent in Edenderry.

St John of God Convent,
built *c.*1916.

The issue of Home Rule was still on the agenda in 1917, and Denis Sheil
and James Colgan attended a national convention in Dublin on 19 April
where Count Plunkett addressed the crowd about Home Rule and Ireland's
participation in a post-war peace conference. The rapid rise of Sinn Féin in
the aftermath of the 1916 rebellion affected Edenderry and in July 1917
a meeting was held to re-establish the old club of Sinn Féin, which had
ceased to exist. At the meeting T.M. Russell of Tullamore addressed the men
and told them that 'the red flame of Erin's name confronts the world once
more'.

Taking the chair, Denis Sheil told the crowd that he was proud to do so
and claimed that Sinn Féin was not a secret society. He said that Mr Dooley
MP had no more right to represent King's County than Paddy Onions had,
and that Onions would never sell out his country like Dooley had so he
was owed an apology, which was met with much laughter. Those who were
present at the meeting of the revitalised Sinn Féin branch at Edenderry
included James Colgan, P. Usher, J. Fox, J. Tiernan, M. Foley, P. Jackson, J.
Beatty, J. Kelly and P. Kenny.[206] The patriotic spirit had been rekindled, it
seemed, as on Decoration Day in July 1917 the Sinn Féin club evoked the
memory of Kearns and Perry by laying wreaths of green, white and orange
on their grave in Monasteroris graveyard. The inscription on the card read
'Three flowers for the graves of 1798, 1848, 1867, 1916. God rest the souls of
our patriotic dead. *Éire Abu*. Edenderry Sinn Féin.'[207]

A dispute amongst several local youths had its conclusion before the 1917
Petty Sessions, which was presided by W.J.H. Tyrell, Denis Fay and Jasper
Joly, and it showed just how complicated this period was. A young girl,
Mary Cooney, had brought before the court four youths: Thomas McGlynn,
Thomas Foran, David Greer and John Reilly, who she accused of throwing

Left: St Mary's Roman Catholic Church, 1917.

Above: Edenderry Sinn Féin raffle ticket, 1917.

stones at her at New Row corner. It was claimed that Cooney was wearing a Union Jack badge on her coat and was on her way to post a letter to her brother who was in the British Army. One of the boys shouted at her, 'Up the rebels!' while Cooney responded with the call, 'Up the khaki and down with the rebels!' What Denis Fay found strange was that some of the boys that stood accused had brothers who were fighting in the British Army. The boys were fined and Fay said that he hoped that Edenderry would long retain its reputation as the quietest town in the country.

The Sinn Féin club in Edenderry was more than a talking shop and published a manuscript journal on a monthly basis, which contained such items as ideas on improving society, Irish history and a poetry section. However, conditions at Edenderry deteriorated as the First World War dragged on, and in January 1918 a serious food shortage was reported. A committee was set up to provide food for those who were badly affected and Fr Murphy warned that if something was not done soon it would be as bad as 'Black 1847' and appealed to the business people of the town.

As early as March 1918 the volunteers were firmly established in Edenderry and were drilling and preparing for confrontation with the British Army. For a town that had supplied so many soldiers to the British war effort, the attitude had reversed and the Nationalist spirit of the 1880s revived. The exertions of men such as George Patterson and the rebel priest Revd Kinsella were surely recalled. On 26 March 1918 an estimated crowd of five to six hundred volunteers were addressed by Fionan Lynch from County Kerry and Michael Foley,

Fr Paul Murphy PP, 1910-33.

the town's 1916 veteran. The RIC, led by Head Constable O'Gara, halted them at the Hibernian Bank and arrested both Foley and Seamus Clarke from Tullamore. An angry mob followed the RIC to the barracks and Constable Flynn was hit with a stone by one of the Sinn Féiners. The volunteers were unarmed and so did not attack the police, and O'Gara issued instructions to clear the streets. Later in the evening in Monasteroris some 300 volunteers drilled and marched without any interference from the RIC.

The proposal of the British Army to introduce conscription in 1918 was heavily opposed in Edenderry and demonstrations against the plan were organised. In May a soldier of the Scottish Horse regiment that was stationed in Edenderry fell from a tree while removing a Republican flag and later died of his injuries. A day of football and hurling organised by the GAA known as 'Gaelic Sunday' was held in August. In September, the imprisonment of Michael Foley for two months in a Belfast jail did not deter the activities of Sinn Féin in Edenderry. Seditious speeches were delivered in March and May of 1919 by J.J. Walsh, Sinn Féin MP for Cork, and Piaras Béaslaí, Sinn Féin MP for East Kerry, who called on the people to disrupt the government by cutting telegraph and railway lines.[208] It seemed Home Rule was no longer what Nationalists wanted and John Kelly, master of the workhouse and chairman of the Sinn Féin club, called on the people of Edenderry to vote for Sinn Féin and break the union. Despite the militant nature that the war was taking, the people of the town still found time to enjoy the Christmas festivities in 1919, when on St Stephens's night a large

St Mary's Roman Catholic Church interior, 1917.

crowd gathered in the town hall for a night of entertainment organised by the Ancient Order of Hibernians. Among those who performed on the night included B. Byrne, J. Montgomery, T. McGuiness and C. Danaher.[209]

Not everyone of this period would have approved of the exertions of the Sinn Féin branch at Edenderry, as the poet 'Seamus from Clonmore' points out in his 1920 poem entitled 'The Foolish Woman'. Perhaps it was some of the local gentry that Haughton was referring to when he wrote:

> There's a woman lives over the way,
> And I'm wondering what is her name,
> No matter whatever goes wrong her excuse is always the same.
> If her laundry fails to get dry she never complains of the rain,
> But mumbles and grumbles aloud, bad less to that horrid Sinn Féin.
>
> If her hen doesn't lay a large egg,
> It's not for want of good food,
> This woman will tell you with pride, she's the best of a very good brood.
> The reason the egg is so small, she'll tell in tones of disdain,
> The hen went out picking one day and plucked up the seed of Sinn Féin'.

If the cat sits and washes her face,
To clean it and look nice, and won't stop her although the place is infested
with mice, she won't chase the pussy away, or say that she's getting to vain,
Oh no, oh no she will quibble and groan, bad less to that horrid Sinn Féin.

If her daughter goes off to a ball,
Half dressed like a heathen Zulu,
And jumps through the foxtrot or jazz as refined as a mad kangaroo,
She won't blame the teaching she got, or the culture from over the main,
Oh no she will grumble and say bad less to that horrid Sinn Féin.

If a star from the heavens fall down,
And the sun didn't shine in the sky,
This woman would seek out a friend and tell her with many a sigh,
That Sinn Féiners were terrible bad, and all for a paltry gain,
They get socks off in wormwood scrubs because they believe in Sinn Féin.

As battalions and units of the IRA began to be established around the country
so too did one at Edenderry. The battalion was led by James Ginger Moran
(who won an All-Ireland football medal with Kildare in 1919), James Farrelly
was Captain and Tommy Grehan was first lieutenant. A council of elders
was also established to give advice and included Sean O'Ceallaigh Sr, James
Colgan, Dick Mangan and Denis Sheil. Writing to the Town Commissioners,
Charles Manners tendered his resignation as he stated that he could no
longer continue to act as Town Clerk because of the militant and Nationalist
nature of the council. This was something that angered the Commissioners
as Manners had already been paid the year's salary in advance.

The town council elections in 1920 were contested both by members of
Sinn Féin and the Labour party, the latter agreeing to sign the Republican
pledge and some even standing aside so that Sinn Féin would gain a majority. In total 600 people were eligible to vote in these elections, and it is
believed as many as 500 turned out to cast their vote on Election Day.[210] In
February 1920 John Kelly was elected as the first Sinn Féin chairman of the
town council. Another member of the town council, Andrew Byrne, had
a lucky escape after a gas explosion at his Railway Bar in February 1920.
Rumours abounded that he had been storing explosives for the IRA, but
none were found when the RIC checked the premises. At this time Byrne

Edenderry IRA members, 1922.

was also chairman of the Edenderry Board of Guardians, whose committee had drastically changed, now comprising of Nationalist members such as J. Moore, F. Mullen, L.H. Malone, D. Sheil and J. Colgan.[211]

Following the resignation of Manners as Town Clerk the council was free to openly express their allegiance and in April 1920 stated that the 'council hereby recognises the authority of Dáil Éireann as the duly elected government of the Irish people and undertake to give effect to all laws passed by same'. A copy of this was even sent to the House of Representatives in the USA. The summer of 1920 saw the volunteers increase their activities, effectively controlling the town, taking such steps as to close all public houses at 9 p.m. every evening and close them completely on Sundays. The post office was raided on 21 June and the sum of £490 taken. This prompted an influx of soldiers and RIC to descend upon the town, as did officials from the GPO, to carry out an investigation. At midnight four men were arrested and the soldiers retired and were billeted at Miss Ball's house at Monasteroris.

The military remained at Monasteroris and set up daily roadblocks at both Monasteroris and Killane crosses, which were necessary steps after the burning of the Rhode and Fahy barracks in August. The IRA at Edenderry was employed in the months of August and September in saving the hay of Dick Mangan of Killane, one of their council of elders who had been arrested and jailed. The Protestant gentry around Edenderry had always

Above: Notice for Iaasc Yodikin *c.*1918.

Right: John Kelly, Master of the Edenderry Workhouse.

feared a backlash from their Nationalist neighbours should there ever be popular unrest in the area, and they experienced such in late 1920. The homes of many of these men such as Wakely in Ballyburley, Rait Kerr at Rathmoyle and Beaumont Nesbitt at Tubberdaly were all raided and arms taken. The military responded by carrying out a swoop on gun licences and no one was exempt from having their guns taken, including Dr Kinsella, T. O'Kearney White and Eugene O'Brien.

Several members of the RIC stationed at Edenderry, including Constables Shanahan, Fitzpatrick and McManus, resigned their posts fearful of the threat posed by the IRA. In September 1920 Constable George Morley, based at the RIC barracks at Clonbullogue, committed suicide, so desperate had his situation become.[212] Clearly in support of the local IRA, Andrew Byrne dismissed Rait Kerr's claim for compensation for the burning of Rhode RIC barracks, throwing the claim form in the bin. The volunteers at Edenderry imposed strict sanctions on goods that were brought into the town and a ban was placed on the purchase of goods from Belfast, as they would not trade with the 'city of medieval bigotry'. In October 1920 volunteers arrested a man at the railway station in Edenderry who had come from Belfast seeking orders and, as the *Leader* commented, he was to say the least, 'ruffled up'.

As with other parts of the country, the winter of 1920/21 saw most of the unrest; ambushes, looting and burning buildings, which was common-

View along the Main Street
*c.*1912.

place in the Edenderry area. The Edenderry Board of Guardians (soon to disband) stated in late 1920 that, 'We hereby sever all connections with the British government and recognise only departments of Dáil Éireann.' There was much excitement in the town when John Kelly, then chairman of Offaly County Council, was arrested at the mart along with James Glynn and Thomas Brerton in November. Previous to this, Kelly's house had been raided on numerous occasions. On one such visit the floorboards were torn up and the ceiling torn down, but nothing could be found to incriminate Kelly or his family. Kelly had incurred the wrath of the RIC and the Black and Tans when, in June 1920 at a meeting of the County Council, he proposed to change the name of King's County to Offaly, because King's County was one of the counties 'bearing the name which shows the trait of the invader' and that it was time to revive the 'ancient and illustrious title of Offaly'. Despite this the people of the town observed the Armistice on 11 November 1920, as the mill's machines stopped and the bells of Castro Petre sounded to remember the town's dead from the 'Great War'.

The military now stationed at Denis Fay's residence at Blundell House raided the workhouse on numerous occasions and took away the meeting books of the board. The local IRA unit was active and blew up many bridges, making the roads impassable for the army and the RIC. Again Michael Foley was the target of the military. He was arrested in February 1921 and sentenced to a further three months imprisonment. His possessions taken on this occasion included a dairy he had kept in 1916 describing his involvement in the activities of Easter Week. Another local arrested was a man named Hughes who was found to be in the possession of a Sinn Féin songbook.[213] In March four men of the Edenderry battalion of the IRA, George Bell, William Coady, James Ryan and Hugh Murphy, were arrested at Cushina Bridge, near Portarlington.[214]

As the war continued social conditions deteriorated and up to sixty men were off work from Aylesbury's. A serious epidemic of influenza and pneumonia made matters worse; one family at the harbour lost two children in the one week to the 'flu. The inhabitants of the town were searched on every occasion possible, be it coming from a dance, mass or the market. A peculiar incident occurred in February 1921 when the residents of the town awoke to see a plane circling the town at a very low level, coming relatively close to the roofs of many houses. This was followed by leaflets being dropped in the town the following Monday, warning people against showing sympathy with the IRA.

Towards the end of February 1921 an ambush on the RIC occurred at Mount Lucas. Constable Doherty and two English officers were wounded and the military, it was said, searched every house in Edenderry, making numerous arrests. A major coup for the army was the arrest of J.J. Sutton, a timber buyer in Aylesbury's Mills, who had been sought for many months for his part in ambushes and drilling in the area. A nervous tension prevailed in the town and many shops remained closed for days, fearful of reprisals from the army. In defiance the IRA fired shots at 2 a.m. in Killane every night that the shops remained closed.

The correspondent for the *Leinster Leader* was not quite his vocal self in this period but did however pass comment on the arrest of a young man named Christopher Kane who was arrested in April 1921 at his home, 'Irish Cottage' on the Tunnel Road. It was later discovered that Kane had in his possession a six-chamber revolver and eighteen rounds of ammunition. The RIC also imposed a ban on people using bicycles from 15 June to 11 July, as trees continued to be felled and the roads blocked around Edenderry. Workers on the railway junction at Edenderry were attacked and their tools taken from them by a party of the IRA. The RIC responded by arresting two brothers named Cleary from Kishawanna, and M. Larkin who was taken from the mill while he worked.[215] Not to be deterred, the IRA launched its most daring attack during the War of Independence at Edenderry, when Blundell House was attacked on the night of 9 June 1921. According to the official Dublin Castle report:

Traps leaving Aylesbury's.

At 2.45 a.m. on Friday a number of armed civilians endeavoured to force an entry to yard of the RIC barracks at Edenderry. The police opened fire and the civilians retreated firing a number of shots back at the barrack. During the exchange Constable Patrick McDonnell was accidentally killed. A few nights ago several RIC while sitting outside the barracks at the hospital were fired at by a number of armed men. None of the police were injured.

The military responded the following day by gathering all the male inhabitants of the town together in the market square, where they took every man's name, address and family details. Some were taken to the Curragh in military lorries. In the hours before the truce was declared in July, Republican and USA flags flew from poles around Edenderry, and armed volunteers raided the home of long time foe Jasper Joly – relieving him of bicycles, cars and money. From the end of April until the truce was signed on 11 July 1921, the people of Edenderry had to endure a curfew, which restricted them from leaving their house between the hours of 9 p.m. and 5 a.m. The last action of the War of Independence occurred with the shooting of Constable Adams outside Williams' shop. The *Leader* reported that it had occurred after the truce although local tradition has it occurring just before it. Adams, who was on his way to do private business, was an Englishman who was married to a woman from Rathangan and he had recently converted to Catholicism. He was shot through the arm and side, which left him paralysed and wheelchair bound. He was later awarded £1,000 compensation at the court in Tullamore.

After the truce was announced in July 1921, open-air concerts, road races and GAA matches were enjoyed by the people once more. The collection

View from the
Hibernian Bank
*c.*1900.

of rates by the Edenderry Town Council proved difficult during the truce
however, and John Kelly wrote to the ratepayers warning them of the consequences of failing to pay. Kelly believed that there was a concerted effort
on the part of certain people to withhold rates.[216] Despite the ceasefire,
the IRA liaison officer reported in late July that the truce was not being
adhered to, as he realised when District Inspector Magnier fled from a
party of the IRA. The liaison officer complained that Magnier and his crew
were fully armed and were, in his opinion, on a reconnaissance mission.[217]
Many of those interned during the War of Independence were not released
until December 1921. A huge crowd gathered in December to welcome J.J.
Sutton and a Mr Cleary from their internment at Rath Camp.[218] At a massive demonstration to celebrate the exertions of the local unit of the IRA,
Fr Paul Murphy thanked Dr Pat McCartan TD for the work he had done
throughout the war. McCartan told the gathering to 'beware of the hoofs
of a horse, the horns of a bull and the smile of an Englishman', because
until the last British soldier was gone from Ireland the country would not
be content. Fr Murphy concluded the speeches with the hope that the
mills would soon be humming and that Edenderry would come back to its
own.[219]

Opposition to the Treaty would soon be made vocal and the horrors of
the Civil War were only around the corner. In January 1922, during the
Treaty debates, the Edenderry Town Council declared that they were in
favour of the terms of the treaty. James Mangan proposed and was seconded
by Bernard McGuiness that:

Jim Farrelly leading the IRA
Easter parade.

We express our complete confidence in the honesty and patriotism of the
members of An Dáil, both those for and against the Treaty; that while we
admit the treaty is not an act of self determination by the Irish people, at the
same time it is no instrument of dishonour achieved as it was after a fight of
tremendous odds against us and can be made the means to freedom in the
fullest sense. For this reason we desire our deputies to vote for its ratification,
and by doing so express the wishes of those for whom they act as deputies,
failure to do this would be misrepresentation, and opposed to the principle of
government by the people.

An advertisement in a local newspaper in November 1921 noting that
Sylvester Rait Kerr was giving up breeding and selling his brood mares,
foals, stallions and saddlery is evidence of the impending threat he envisaged
from the IRA.[220]

Aftermath: Civil War and compensation

The locals believed that once they saw off the Black and Tans, that they would never experience a poor day again. The break up of the Downshire estate, along with the other smaller estates around Edenderry, was the topic of much discussion after the Treaty and indeed throughout the 1920s. Many people were preoccupied with compensations from hardships brought about by the War of Independence and the Civil War; indeed many of these claims were debated in the Dáil by local representatives. The number of claims raised in the Dáil would indicate that Edenderry was troubled by the Civil War, which raged from June 1922-May 1923.

As the Civil War raged in Ireland, the people of Edenderry actively sought to bring about the final settlement in the purchase of their holdings from the Marquess of Downshire. On 12 January 1923 a meeting of the tenants was told that the Edenderry Town Tenants' Committee was in the position to purchase the town hall for £500. A petition of over 616 signatures and delivered to the 'Most honourable Marquess of Downshire' asking him not to consider an offer from five gentlemen (only one of whom was a tenant) to purchase the town hall. Among those present that denounced the actions of the men trying to buy the town hall were Daniel Aylesbury, John Kelly, chairman of Offaly County Council, J.F. Gill and P. Murphy. The meeting concluded, resolving that 'the town hall should be at all times the property of the people'. Trustees for the town hall were also nominated on the night, including: A.P. Fay, William O' K. White, T.F. O'Toole, D. Aylesbury Sr, A. Williams, W. Corrigan, J.P.H. Patterson, J.M. Crowe, H. Farrelly, F.B. O'Toole, M. Delaney, J.F. Gill, E. Wall, James O'Neill, James Mangan, P.

Murphy, D. Corrigan, P. Mooney, P.J. Ivory, C. Dunne, J. Earle, T. Donahue and J. Kelly.[221]

In July 1922, National Army troops stationed in Edenderry were called to Drehid, Carbury, where a party of Irregulars were in hiding. After a gun battle seven Irregulars were arrested and taken back to Edenderry.[222] The funeral of Michael Collins was observed in Edenderry in late August 1922, when the all the shops closed as a mark of respect and many people travelled to Glasnevin for the funeral. A national school teacher in Castlejordan, T.F. McAuliffe, was quoted as having met Collins a few weeks prior to his death and that Collins had told him that Edenderry was 'one bright spot'.[223] The fighting quickly resumed however, and the Edenderry barracks (located at the workhouse) was attacked for the sixth time in August when eight men tried to rush the sentry and gain entrance. In the same week Miss Ball's residence at Mount Lucas was broken into by four masked men who tied her to the gate of the house. Owing to the ongoing fighting and the fact that fifteen bridges in the locality had been blown up, Aylesbury's suspended work at their factory.[224]

The maintaining of law and order at Edenderry was helped by the arrival of the Civic Guard (forerunner to An Garda Síochána) in December 1922. Six men were stationed at the harbour in Mrs O'Brien's house, formerly John Keating's. They were quickly called into action when a dispute broke out between E.B. Smyth and the Jellico family at Ballycolgan. The Civic Guard Sergeant Michael Comer arrested a Mr Walsh, nephew of Charles and Pat Jellico, for illegal entry onto land at Ballycolgan and brought him before the courts.[225]

Compensation

Many volunteers from Edenderry took an active part in the Civil War, mostly on the part of the Provisional Government or 'Free Staters'. The financial chaos that the country was experiencing, exacerbated by the Civil War, meant that even as late as 1925 many of the volunteers from Edenderry were still seeking payment for services rendered with the National Army. In January 1924 Laois/Offaly TD Liam O'Daimhin enquired in the Dáil as to the wages that were due to Patrick Mooney of Blundell Street for his service in the National Army.[226] Similarly O'Daimhin enquired about the dependents allowance promised to Thomas Williams of the Tunnel Road who had served from May 1922 to September 1923. The President ruled that all money due had been paid to Mrs Williams.[227] The plight of Edward Cummins was also raised in the Dáil, who, after serving in the 3rd Wexford Brigade, had no income and now faced the prospect of relying on the generosity of friends and family. It was argued that he would soon have to be admitted to the workhouse in Tullamore if he did not receive compensation.[228] There were several other men from Edenderry who, having left employment to assist the provisional government 'in protecting the lives and property of the people of the area', sought compensation for that service.[229]

The business and tradesmen of the town were also affected by the Civil War and its calamity. As late as 1925 Mr McGuinness of Main Street, who had carried out work for members of the National Army, was still owed £2 20s 6d.[230] Another man named Thomas Gorman sought pay of 3s per day for work carried out at the workhouse, which was used as the barracks for the National Army. The work included repairs to be carried out by those in charge: Flanagan, Dowling, Hamilton, Kenny and Kelly.[231] The arrears owed to M.P. O'Brien for goods supplied to the Army in 1921 were also disputed. Speaking in the Dáil, P.J. Egan asked when O' Brien would be reimbursed £186 14s. The President ruled that the claims were made during a period when money, 'cannot be discharged out of funds voted by the Dáil for the maintenance of the Army'.[232]

The gentry around Edenderry, themselves victims of the War of Independence and the Civil War reprisals, also sought compensation for their losses. The manner in which J.J. Robison of Newberry Hall was treated was indicative of this period. The National Army had commandeered his motor car in August 1922 and it was found in January 1923 as a complete wreck in Edenderry Barracks. The sum of £200 was offered to Robinson despite it having cost £830 to buy in 1920.[233] E.J. Beaumont Nesbitt of Tubberdaly House was treated in the same manner when trying to seek compensation for furniture destroyed in early 1921 when the IRA sent his house up in flames. The IRA forced Nesbitt (who, during the previous ten years, had buried his wife and lost three sons in the Great War) out of the country, and he never returned. He left his compensation battle in the hands of William O'Kearney White, the Edenderry solicitor whose father Terence had been the torment of the landlords in the past.[234] Others who were seeking compensation included Charles Nelson who was seeking compensation after being forced to leave the locality,[235] as was Thomas O'Brien who had his vehicle commandeered in October 1922.[236]

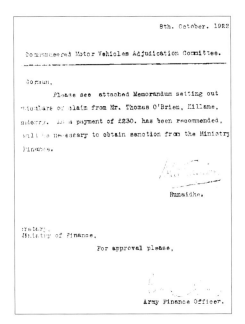

8th. October. 1923

Commandeered Motor Vehicles Adjudication Committee.
_____

  Gorman,
          Please see attached Memorandum setting out
particulars of claim from Mr. Thomas O'Brien, Killane,
Edenderry. As a payment of £230. has been recommended,
will be necessary to obtain sanction from the Ministry
Finance.

                                    Runaidhe.

  Secretary,
  Ministry of Finance.
                     For approval please,

                          Army Finance Officer.

Civil War compensation claim, 1923.

Other innocents who experienced losses during the Civil War included John Gill of Ticknevin, who had his bicycle taken from him by Commandant Powell of the National Troops from Edenderry on 3 July 1922.[237] The Officer Commanding of the Edenderry troops, Patrick Hannon, confiscated a new Royal Enfield bicycle belonging to Joseph Ennis valued at £12 10s. After various enquiries no evidence could be found to help locate the bicycle.[238]

The Civil War, which lasted from June 1922-May 1923, did affect the town of Edenderry and its environs. As well as the compensation claims listed above, other incidents occurred which show that the people of the area were affected by the Civil War, despite the fact that Offaly remained relatively quiet throughout this period. In January 1923 the ex-officers and volunteers of the Edenderry 4th Battalion No. 1 Offaly Brigade met in the town hall in an effort to restore the peace. Former brigade adjutant George Bell presided at the meeting where a committee proposing to act in the interests of Ireland formed a committee of pre-truce IRA men's association. The committee elected included Bell as president, Hugh Murphy (formerly battalion quartermaster) as secretary and Thomas Farrell (former Intelligence officer) as treasurer. Amongst the committee's first actions was to provide a guard of honour for the funeral of James Martin of Drehid, Carbury, who had been killed by accidental discharge at Kingscourt in County Cavan.[239] In February, the committee also appealed for the Irregulars to lay down their arms, and thanked the people of north Offaly for their support in the recent Anglo-Irish war.[240]

The death of Thomas Kane at Newtown, Rhode, in April 1923 evokes the saddest memory of the Civil War period at Edenderry. Kane, who had fought in the 'Great War' later joined the National Army in the Curragh and was stationed in Wexford during the Civil War. He had absented himself from the Army without permission and was being sought by National troops when he was cornered at Newtown on 7 April. The inquest into his death conducted by Mr T. Conway at Tullamore Hospital stated that he had been shot in the hip and stomach while trying to flee the Free State troops. He had been in hiding at Sheil's house at Mount Lucas for some weeks before the National Army were informed of his location. Witnesses at Edenderry claimed that he had been wounded in Wexford during the fighting there, while Dr Meagher of Daingean stated that the victim had told him, while being treated, that it was foolish on his part to run but that he had never heard the cry of halt before been shot. Despite this, the verdict of the court was that it had been a genuine military action and offered sympathy to his family. The *Leinster Leader* described his funeral at Drumcooley, which was attended by huge numbers, and noted that his father was 'a humble hard-working man who is well known in the town'.[241]

The break-up of landed estates

By 1914 holdings worth £116,137 on the Downshire estate had been sold to the tenants. However in 1922 Downshire was still in possession of 6,730 acres, but most of which was bog and only the ground rents in the town remained to the former landlord. The Palmer estate at Rahan, Edenderry was acquired in 1936 by the Land Commission, which entailed some 980 acres.[242] Other local estates had not been divided by 1936; twelve years after division had first begun. These included the Smith, Dames, Weld and O'Brien estates. The division of the Ball estate at Edenderry had taken place during 1928 and 1929 but in 1931 some tenants were still unhappy with proceedings there.[243] It was claimed that there were people in Edenderry living in stables and that, appallingly, it was members of the Town Commissioners who owned these stables.[244] Other estates that the people were wishing to have broken-up included the 291 acres owned by Paul Gill at Ballycolgan, the Baker estate at Monasteroris and 274 acres at Ballydermot.

Train derailed
by the IRA
at Edenderry,
March 1923.

The decline of the Gentry

The landed gentry in the area around Edenderry were the biggest losers in
the War of Independence and the Civil War; their livelihoods were disturbed
and the way of life they had enjoyed for so long was destroyed, never to
return. But this decline had been slowly occurring over the previous forty
years; the sale of estates after the Wyndham Land Act of 1903 and fatalities
in the 'Great War' exacerbated their demise. The landlords had always feared
a backlash from the locals and during the War of Independence and Civil
War many used the civil unrest in the country to settle old scores. On 27
July 1922 Sylvester Rait Kerr of Rathmoyle House, a Justice of the Peace
and former member of the Edenderry Board of Guardians, was found dead
on the front lawn of his home. Fearing the backlash of the local IRA whom
he believed to be on the way to torch his mansion, Rait Kerr committed
suicide. He had been an extensive landowner and large employer in the
area, leaving an estate valued at £52,225. The Dames' estate at Greenhills
suffered the same fate as Tubberdaly and Rathmoyle. On 6 February 1923
Greenhills House, the residence of Desmond Longworth Dames, was completely destroyed. His grandmother, aged eighty-two, her daughter and two
female maids were present when a party of twenty Irregulars (only two of
whom were masked) attacked the house. They claimed it was a reprisal for
the execution of Patrick Gerethy, a local who had been executed by the Free
State troops in Portlaoise. They allowed the Dames family ten minutes to
clear the house before it was set alight. Commenting on the burning of the
Dames and Wakely homes, the *Leinster Leader* asked, 'What is becoming of

Rathmoyle House.

Ireland? The kindly folk like the Wakelys and the Dames have their homes
burnt to the ground.' The Edenderry Rural District Council received a
subsequent claim of £43,000 for the burning of Greenhills House.[245]

The destruction of the 'big houses' in the locality during both the War
of Independence and the Civil War leaves a stain on this period. The owners of Greenhills, the Dames family, had a long connection with the area;
indeed Francis Longworth Dames had been instrumental in the setting
up of the Edenderry Poor Law Union and for providing relief during the
famine. Likewise the Nesbitts of Tubberdaly had provided much needed
employment in the area and in 1877 Ms Catherine Downing Nesbitt had
provided £10,000 for the construction of the railway from Edenderry to
Enfield. Tubberdaly House was burned on 15 April 1923 at 2 a.m. when
raiders ordered the servants out before torching the mansion with petrol
and home-made bombs. An attempt was also made on 6 December 1922
to burn Ballindoolin House; six bullet holes still remain in the wall today.
Trying to understand why his house had been attacked, William J.H. Tyrell
claimed that it may have been because he was a Justice of the Peace for
forty-eight years or that he 'was always ready to help the government or
because he had a son in the British Army'.[246] In the minority, the gentry of
the locality were driven bag and baggage out of the area never to return,
as Revd John Wyer's comments some forty years previous were realised.
Another example of the inhumanity shown by the North Offaly IRA at
this time was the murder of Special Constable John Hannon. Taken from his
home near Rathangan in July 1920, his body was discovered in a bog hole
between Edenderry and Philipstown some eleven months later. According

Ballyburley
House, after
being burnt in
1923.

to the *Leinster Leader,* Hannon had written to his family during his captivity, which indicates that he was held hostage and was executed before the truce was ushered in. His wife was later awarded £2,600 as compensation for her loss.[247]

Conclusion

In 1929 the Edenderry Town Commissioners finally succeeded in purchasing the town hall for the people of the town. A local reporter noted that the 'transfer will revive memories to Edenderry folk who remember the days when the fine stately building was called the market house and courthouse but rarely the town hall. The vast majority lived without ever seeing its fine ballroom. Today the town hall is now the people's property.' On 24 January 1945 the town hall was gutted by fire and subsequently rebuilt. Since then the people of the town have little to do with their town hall, instead Offaly County Council administer affairs of the county from there.

Many people continued paying a ground rent on holdings in the town of Edenderry to the successors of the Marquess of Downshire. A Mr and Mrs E. Merrey of Blessington were the last of Downshire's agents to collect rent in this area, and George Russell was the last gamekeeper with responsibility for the large numbers of game on the bogs surrounding Edenderry. Local

Edenderry Town Hall on fire, 1945.

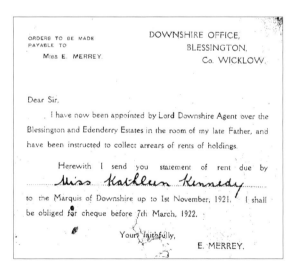

Downshire Estate bill, 1922.

people remember Sir John Maffey, British Ambassador to Ireland during the Second World War, shooting for game at the Derries where local men were employed as beaters, hunting out pheasant and grouse. In 1963 the then Marquess of Downshire was still contributing £2 10s 0d to Revd B.E. Pemberton for the upkeep of Castro Petre church in Edenderry.

Today little evidence remains of the improvements made by the 3rd Marquess of Downshire, only a small number of the houses that he built

IRA memorial (full length).

to improve the appearance of the town remain. The fine monument on the top of the long church walk at Castro Petre retains a link with the former owners of the soil and to our own past. Blundell House, now a private residence, still retains its elegance, but one wonders how the people of the town from 1820-1920 would have looked with scorn on the occupants of the house. Weather-beaten and forgotten, the grave of George Patterson has failed to become a lasting memorial or place of retreat for the Nationalists of the area.

As more and more historians reassess important periods in Irish history, such as the War of Independence and the Civil War, Nationalist rhetoric can be brushed aside and the period in question examined properly. Edenderry must reassess its own historical past and realise that what we once believed to be 'glorious and heroic' events include many hidden stories and dishonourable deeds. When standing in St Mary's Roman Catholic Cemetery at the memorial erected at Easter 1960 in memory of the local volunteers of the IRA, one can not help but wonder if a similar monument will ever be erected commemorating the town's 'Great War' of 1914-18 dead. These men deserve to be remembered.

'Does it matter which side fired the shot,
Or what sergeant barked the order.
Was pain felt less at Boland's Mills
Than in the trenches of the Somme'.[248]

Snippets from the past

Throughout the course of research for this book, several incidents and events at Edenderry have come to attention, which, while not meriting inclusion in the main text, merit inclusion here. Readers may find them interesting.

The Times, 16 November 1816
On 11 November 1816 it was reported that a hot air balloon had landed near to Edenderry after setting off from Richmond Barracks in Dublin.

King's County Chronicle, 24 December 1845
A farmer named Carroll from Edenderry was sent to gaol for a month for stealing fifty-three ball cartridges from two soldiers of the 41st regiment who are stationed in Edenderry. Carroll was found guilty of robbing the two men while they were drinking in a local public house.

King's County Chronicle, 6 January 1848
At the Edenderry Assizes, Bridget Reilly and Anne Weir were found guilty of stealing a watch and chain from Thomas O'Brien on 6 December 1847. Weir was sentenced to seven years' transportation.

The Times, 25 January 1862
The very first post office in Edenderry is to be opened on 3 February 1862.

Leinster Leader, 21 January 1882: Emergency expedition to Edenderry
Lieutenant Ford of the Rifle brigade and an escort travelling by jaunting car
at 2 a.m. Saturday morning to inspect military posts at Grange Castle and
Ballinabracky collided with a donkey and cart. The car overturned and the
soldiers got a roll in the mud. The donkey carried on, proud of his feat of
knocking a few British soldiers.

Leinster Leader, 20 February 1886
A Loyalist called Sam Hurst was fined half a crown for beating a man to the
ground. All you have to be is a Loyalist and you receive impunity

Leinster Leader, 16 February 1887
The editor of the *Leinster Leader* received a letter from Joseph E. Patterson,
Australian Lodge, Edenderry. Patterson stated that he had lived in Australia
where the savages were supposed to grow hair on their teeth, but even if
they do they get a fair trial. The Australians helped England in the Egyptian
war – and he believed that Ireland would do the same if they were let. We
are treated like dogs tied to a chain and beaten by the English according to
Patterson.

Leinster Leader, 20 August 1887
The Edenderry National League Band undertook an excursion to Lake
Belvedere near Mullingar on Saturday last. They were accompanied by their
efficient bandmaster Mr Murphy, Mr McGuinness and Michael Costello.
They left Edenderry at 7.30 a.m. in five carts and toured Westmeath. They
saw Mullingar and in the evening played in Rhode on the way home.

Leinster Leader, 24 December 1887
On 13 December Revd A. Hume PP, Rhode was buried. A large number of
Protestants were there in attendance at the Mass. Capt Dames of Greenhills
House sent a beautiful wreath in the shape of the cross. Hume was fourteen
years a priest in Rhode and had spent forty-seven years in the priesthood.

The Times, 3 February 1888
On 30 January 1888 from the accidental discharge of his gun while stalk-
ing wild geese, Francis Talbot Longworth Dames, Captain Royal Artillery,
aged twenty-seven and eldest son of Capt Longworth Dames JP DL of
Greenhills, died.

Leinster Leader, 4 February 1893
Disgraceful scenes are reported from Edenderry where a wedding took place on a Sunday. The wedding party went about the town shouting and blowing horns. The reporter has never heard of this happening before.

Leinster Leader, 17 June 1893
A young man named Frank Higgins was drowned, while another named Kenny escaped at Blackbushes, a local swimming spot along the Grand Canal at Edenderry. A local man named Michael Mallon rescued Kenny and then dived in for the body of Higgins. He is to be given a medal by the people of the town.

Leinster Leader, 19 August 1893
Bill Davey rescued Mary Connor, a young girl who fell into the Grand Canal at Edenderry. In 1882 when only fifteen he rescued Philip Kennedy, a friend. In 1885 he rescued William Haughey at Blackbushes. In 1891 he rescued a young girl named Haughton.

Midland Tribune, 20 December 1902
A burning has been reported during the week, from Mount Prospect, near Edenderry, between thirty-five and forty tons of hay being destroyed. Mr T. O' K. White, the owner, has lodged a claim, for malicious injury to the amount of £105. When the Edenderry R.D.C. No. 1 Council was confronted with the claim, the members did not know how it would be defended, he being their solicitor. Mr White was presented by Mr Moore, and after some consideration, the District Council entrusted their defence to Mr Stephen Browne of Naas.

March 1905
Limerick man Norman Palmer set up the Drumcooley Peat Moss Works in 1905 when his factory at Goldenbridge was burned. The new factory was at the Downshire Bridge along the Grand Canal near Edenderry.

Taken from C.P. Kingston, The Book of the Administration of King's County
In 1911 the following people in the Edenderry area owned motor cars: Daniel Aylesbury (two cars), M.P. O'Brien, Samuel Clarke, John J. Kinsella, Aylesbury brothers, E.J. Beaumont Nesbitt, Edward B. Smyth, Arthur Williams, Judge Wakely and Sylvester Rait Kerr. The UPS were the only

shop in Edenderry entitled to sell explosives in 1911, while R.W. Potterton, James Fox and John Pelin had the right to sell poisonous substances. The following were elected to co-ordinate the Old Age Pensions scheme which came into being in 1911: James Reilly, Revd Paul Murphy, Revd R.H. Bodel, Revd M. Hipwell, Denis Fay, Denis Sheil and Matthew Moore.

Leinster Leader, 18 June 1913
The following have contributed to the building of the new church in Edenderry by Fr Paul Murphy. Patrick Mulvin, Rooske, has given £60 to pay for four Stations of the Cross; Terence Groome gave £15 for one cross, as did Michael Byrne, Main Street. John and Edward Lennon of Ballykilleen and James Delaney of the Harbour paid for the altar of the Blessed Virgin. The people of the Tunnel Road and the cottages gave £6 and the Junior Hurling club gave 6s. Mrs Thomas O'Connor of the Harbour Bar collected £1 6s 6d in a box left in the shop.

Leinster Leader, 13 April 1913
Head Constable Wolfe and Sub Constable Comiskey went to Scotland, where from Motherwell they conveyed back to Edenderry Joseph Burke where he is remanded on bail.

Leinster Leader, 29 January 1916
The Petty Sessions at Edenderry imposed a months jail on the 'greatest rowdy in Dublin', John Hickey an itinerant who was arrested after smashing twenty-eight windows in the Universal Providing Stores.

Leinster Leader, 24 March 1917
The death has occurred of Dick Magill who passed away in the infirmary. His father had been caretaker in the Town Hall in years previous. The Magills were shoemakers and were always well dressed and as a result was often mistaken to be the Marquess of Downshire.

Leinster Leader, 18 May 1918
The death occurred of Nicholas Mullen in Aylesbury's, after a saw had cut him over the heart. He was only twenty years of age and a member of the Sinn Féin club and the Volunteers. He was buried in Ballymacwilliam.

Leinster Leader, 20 July 1918
At Aylesbury's mills 112 are reported to be suffering from influenza, which is rampant in the town.

Leinster Leader, 2 October 1920
Michael Murphy of Edenderry is seeking £50 compensation after someone tied a tin can to his donkey's tail causing the donkey to bolt from the field in Monasteroris before crashing into a stone wall, causing fatal damage.

Leinster Leader, 5 February 1921
The body of Patrick O'Toole of Kishawanna, a local coach maker, was taken from a drain close to the River Boyne. He had slipped on loose stones when travelling into Edenderry in the dark. He was seventy-three years of age.

The Times, 22 March 1927
Reporting the death of Mr Charles Colley Palmer DL JP (82) of Rahan House who had property in Great Britain and the Irish Free State worth £36,036.

The Times, 19 April 1928
Tenants moving under the Land Act settlement from the Dingle peninsula to Edenderry. Some thirty-five persons with 350 livestock left by a special train of 37 wagons. A new house has been provided for every family, and 1,000 acres divided among them and each has been given 17-40 cattle.

The Times, 24 March 1930
Reporting the death of Mr John Jerome Kinsella, Edenderry, medical practitioner whose personal estate in England and the Irish Free State is worth £8,549.

Dáil Éireann Volume 34: 2 April 1930
Speaking in Edenderry on the 23 March 1930, Deputy Sean Lemass said, 'That it is the purpose of Fianna Fáil to convince the people that economic prosperity and national progress … which in turn cannot be achieved until degrading obligations of the Treaty are removed.' In Offaly, particularly the Edenderry area Lemass commented that there are:

> … a number of solicitors who have interested themselves deeply on behalf
> of the landlords in days gone by. When the commissioners notify landown-

ers of their intention to acquire land these solicitors and their advisers and friends with powerful influences behind them, gather together in a hall in the town and decide to put their heads together with a view to beating the Town Commissioners.

Dáil Éireann Volume 48: 12 July 1933, Oral Answers
In the Dáil on 12 July 1933 the issue of a Peace Commissioner in Edenderry was raised. Speaking for Dr O'Higgins, a Mr Morrissey asked the Minister for Justice was he aware that Mr George O'Connell had been appointed a Peace Commissioner; and if he had, was he further aware that under the heading of Irish Republican Army in the *Offaly Independent*, 13 May 1933 the name of George O'Connell, Edenderry appeared as one of those authorised to accept recruits for the Irish Republican Army, and if full enquiries were made before the appointment to the Peace Commissionership was made.

Appendices

Appendix 1

The following is a list of some people who emigrated from Edenderry to the United States of America between the years 1897–1904 and who passed through the famous Ellis Island in New York.

Name	Year of Emigration	Age
Jennie Dunne	1897	25
John Dunne	1897	26
Maria Dunne	1904	26
Mary A. Dunne	1899	25
Michael Dunne	1900	26
Michael Dunne	1899	19
Francis W. Delaney	1904	40
Jane Carroll	1902	16
Dennis Carty	1903	35
Daniel Daly	1898	58
Edward Daly	1898	15
Ellen Daly	1898	21
Margaret Daly	1898	50

Detail on IRA Memorial in St
Mary's Cemetery.

Mary Daly	1898	14
Patrick Daly	1898	17
Annie Dempsey	1897	22
James Dempsey	1897	24
Joseph Dempsey	1901	21
Patrick Dempsey	1897	26
Thomas Dempsey	1902	23
Lawrence Ennis	1901	27
Thomas M. Farrell	1904	22
Thomas W. Farrell	1903	21
Michael Fitzsimons	1903	22
Peter Kelly	1904	54

Appendix 2

The members of the A. Coy 4th Battalion Offaly Brigade Irish Republican
Army 1916-1921 at Edenderry. The memorial was erected at Easter 1960 in
memory of the deceased members of the battalion.

P. Maher
H. Murphy
T. Wyer
M. Larkin
S. Crinnion
J. Giles
T. Denehan
J. Kelly
H. Butler
R. Davy
B. Dean
D. Corrigan
C. Pentony
M. Behan
G. Bell
P. McEntee
J. Earle
P. Corrigan
M. Clarke
S. O'Kelly
C. Kane
T. Grehan
P. Mullen
J. Farrelly
James Moran
T. Farrell
P. Cullen
W. Cooney
J. Mangan
J. Daly
H. Doyle
W. Coady

IRA Memorial at
St Mary's Cemetery,
Edenderry.

J. Mullen

F. Sullivan

S. Sutton

J. Keyes

W. McEvoy

J. McNally

W. Davy

M. Foran

M. Flynn

J. Judge

J. McCormack

E. O'Connell

J. Fitzsimons

J. Fury

W. Reddy

J. Bergin

H. Donohue

Cumann na mBan

Jane Davy Moran

Kitty White Doyle

M. McCann Farrelly

Reverse of Private Nolan's WWI medal.

Appendix 3

The following is a list of those who contributed to the Prisoners' Maintenance Fund in 1882 in the parish of Edenderry. George Patterson had been a prisoner in 1881 in Kilmainham Gaol.

Revd M. Wall PP, E. Pelin, Jnr, J. Mulvin, M. Delaney, P. Foran, P. Kennedy, T. O'K. White, P.J. Delaney, W. Hanlon, Revd J. Wyer CC, J. Heneghan, R. Brophy, J. Furey, J. Mulvin, P. Fay, T. Clarke, P. Ennis, Doctor Duignan, C. Jellico, E. O'Brien, J. Brophy, Alex Walsh, M. Costello, G. Hackett, H. Farrell, M. Byrne, P. Whelan, M. McNamara, J. Patterson, J. Farrell, J. Delaney, T. O'Toole, T. Farrell, D. Sheil, T. March, T. Whelan, H. Byrne, J. Mulvin, F. Mulvin, P. Bennet, J. Delaney, D. Farrell, Mrs Dillon, J. Flanagan, J. Fay, P. Scully, M. Delany, J. Kennedy, J. Campbell, P. Galvin, P. McGuinness, Mrs H. Farrell, Miss Kennedy, Mrs Finlay, P. Brien, J. Stanton, J. Ennis, H. McGuinness, P. Behan, P. Jellico, J. Ryan, W. Mulligan, L. Connors, J. Mooney, J. Leonard, D. Redmond, T. McGuinness, T. Flood, T. Reilly, J. Donegan, J. Reddy, C. Donaghue, J. Whelan, B. Byrne, N. Cully, P. Dunne, N. O'Toole, Mrs J. Moore, Mrs English, Mrs Kavanagh, Miss Casey, Mrs Brophy, Mrs Mahon, Miss Shaugnessy, Miss Flanagan, Miss Lennon, Miss Cosgrave, Mrs Owens, Mrs Rooney, Mrs Groome, M. Whelan, J. Gray, T. Doyle, D. Kennedy and Mrs N. O'Toole.

Appendix 4

The following is a list of some of those from the Edenderry area who served in the British Army 1783-1918.

  1. Joseph Fyans 1813-21
  2. Peter Walsh 1824-1831
  3. Thomas McLarney 1822-43
  4. Christopher Bonney 1820-1830
  5. James Moran 1807- 1814
  6. John Lenihan 1814-21
  7. John Maxwell 1783-1818
  8. Thomas Lennox 1814-34
  9. Michael Fogarty 1806-33
  10. Patrick Maguire 1825-44
  11. William Harlin, discharged 27/11/1846.
  12. Philip Adams 1827-48
  13. John Johnston 1810-39
  14. Laurence Shields 1827-46
  15. William Walsh, Monasteroris 1808-26
  16. John Hynes, Monasteroris 1826-41
  17. James Ash, Monasteroris 1803-22
  18. Stephen Monaghan 1803-29
  19. Edward Cooley 1848-50
  20. William Dennison 1825-48
  21. James Connell 1826-37
  22. George Patterson 1840-53
  23. James Early 1846-49
  24. Francis Barber 1821-39
  25. Henry Fyans 1827- 49
  26. Thomas White 1825-44
  27. John Heeney 1806-29
  28. Edward Lynch 1808-16
  29. Garrett Walsh 1828-51
  30. John Malone 1799-1825
  31. William Kennedy 1791-1802
  32. William Keane 1809-1812
  33. Private James Cullen (No. 13032) Royal Dublin Fusiliers 6th Battalion

who was killed in the Balkans on the 8/12/1915.

34. Private James Cassidy (No.15557), Royal Dublin Fusiliers 6th Battalion, enlisted in Naas, killed in action in the Balkans 3/10/1916.

35. Private James Cronin (No.74010), Royal Welsh Fusiliers, enlisted in Naas, formerly of the Royal Dublin Fusiliers (No.10327), killed in Egypt 21/10/1918.

36. Private Joseph Brennan (No.5350), Royal Dublin Fusiliers 2nd Battalion, enlisted in Naas, killed in Flanders 15/02/1915.

37. Corporal Reginald James Hinksman (No.16802), Royal Irish Rifles 1st Battalion, born in Sheffield but was living in Edenderry, enlisted in Birr, died in Flanders 7/2/1916.

38. Private James Carroll (No.3405), Royal Dublin Fusiliers 2nd Battalion, enlisted in Carlow, died in Flanders 24/2/1916.

39. Private Patrick Mahon (No.20603), Machine Gun Corps Infantry, enlisted in Tullamore, died of wounds in Flanders 18/3/1916.

40. Private Joseph E. Wright (No.9487), Royal Dublin Fusiliers 2nd Battalion, enlisted in Naas, killed in action in Flanders, 19/3/1916.

41. Private William Carroll (No.9486), Royal Dublin Fusiliers 1st Battalion, enlisted in Naas, died of wounds in Flanders 10/5/1916.

42. Private George William Nelson (No.18092), Royal Inniskilling Fusiliers 9th Battalion, enlisted in Boyle, killed in Flanders 1/7/1916.

43. Michael Dunford (No.5098), Prince of Wales Leinster Regiment (Royal Cavaliers) 2nd Battalion, born in Duagh Co. Kerry, was living in Edenderry, killed in Flanders 24/1/1917.

44. Private Patrick Bryan (No.5100) Prince of Wales Leinster Regiment, died of wounds in Flanders 1/8/1917.

45. Samuel Robinson, Household Cavalry and Cavalry of the Line (yeomanry and imperial Camel Corps) (No.85) born in Seagoe, Co. Down, living in Edenderry, enlisted in Portarlington, died in Flanders 9/8/1917.

46. Cecil Quinn (No.29473), Royal Dublin Fusiliers born in Ballyshannon, Co. Donegal, enlisted in Glasgow, killed in Flanders 5/10/1917.

47. Pat Connell (No.36409) Machine Gun Corps, infantry battalion, formerly of the Royal Irish Regiment (No.9891), enlisted in Dublin, died France 30/11/1917.

48. Private Thomas Shaugnessy (No.15737) born in Rathangan, living in Edenderry and enlisted in Naas, killed in Flanders 25/3/1918.

49. Private Thomas Gill (No.11511) Royal Irish Regiment 2nd Battalion, enlisted in Tullamore, killed in Flanders 20/7/1918.

50. Pat Quinn (No.124679), Machine Gun Corps Infantry, formerly N Staffs Regiment (No.37155), enlisted in Dundee, killed in France 12/8/1918.

51. Thomas Fulton (No.5721) Royal Dublin Fusiliers 1st Battalion, enlisted in Stirling, died in Gallipoli 11/12/1915.

52. Laurence Broughall (No.5006), Royal Muster Fusiliers 6th Battalion, enlisted in Naas, formerly No.16586 of the Royal Dublin Fusiliers, died of wounds at Gallipoli 9/8/1915.

53. William Charles Rait Kerr (died at Ypres 10 November 1914).[249]

54. Laurence McNamee.

55. James Fulton (killed in the 1916 Rising).

56. John McCann (killed in 1914 in France).

57. Joseph McGuinness

58. Bernard Mulrein

59. Patrick Behan (reported dead in May 1917).

60. John Quinn

61. James Smith

62. Capt. Sylvester Cecil Rait Kerr (died at Veldlock 13 May 1915).[250]

63. Christopher Traynor

64. Edward Traynor

65. George Walker

66. Patrick Blong (died in France 1914).

67. Jack Hackett from Ballindoolin (killed in Belgium in October 1918).

68. Michael McGuire (reported to have been captured by the Germans in May 1918).[251]

69. Alexander McBride (died in July 1918).[252]

70. Henry O'Gara (captured by the Germans, July 1918).[253]

71. Laurence Bell and John Webb of the Tunnel Road, Edenderry, reported to be recovering from injuries in July 1918.[254]

72. Private Thomas Burnell (reported wounded in November 1916).[255]

73. WH Beaumont-Nesbitt (killed 27 November 1917).[256]

74. Lieutenant R.A. Hamilton (a doctor in Edenderry promoted to Captain in January 1915).[257]

75. Private Thomas Kane and Private J. Murray (reported to be wounded in August 1916).[258]

76. Lieutenant St Clair Lang, Munster Fusiliers (reported to have died in April 1917 of pneumonia).[259]

77. Edward Graham (died in May 1917).[260]

78. William Odlum of the Irish Guards.[261]

"Rebel" Volunteer Dead.

Mr. Wm. McEvoy, 60, who died at his cottage, Drumcooley, Edenderry, last week was a member of the Sinn Fein Volunteers, who broke away from the Volunteer movement established by the late Mr. John Redmond, M.P., Leader of the Irish Parliamentary Party. Deceased was a very quiet, decent man, whose eyesight had been failing for years until he was almost blind.

Everyone liked and esteemed poor 'Bill" McEvoy who was an industrious, upright and honest Irishman. The funeral from St. Mary's Church to Monasteroris Cemetery on Saturday was very representative. Very Rev. Dr. Tierney, P.P., officiated at the graveside. His daughter, Mrs. Farrell, was chief mourner.

Newspaper obituary for William McEvoy (April 1941).

79. Private Jack Connolly, Tunnel Road, Edenderry.
80. Patrick Nestor (killed 18 March 1916 in Lijssenthoek, Belgium).
81. James Cox (No.21553) Royal Dublin Fusiliers 1st Battalion, born in Rhode, enlisted in Coatbridge, died at Flestel 27/3/1916.
82. Sergeant Michael O'Rourke (No.A/8009) Cameronians Scottish Rifles 5/6 Battalions, born in Rhode, enlisted in Loughgelly, killed in action 8/5/1918.
83. E.W. Bowler, Machine Gun Corps (Infantry), died 25/11/1916.
84. James Murray, Boer War of 1899-1902.
85. George Gray, Boer War of 1899-1902.
86. Thomas Stapleton, Boer War of 1899-1902.
87. John Fulton, Boer War of 1899-1902.
88. Private Gowran, Edenderry was killed in the Boer War of 1899-1902.[262]
89. Sergeant Matthew Boyle killed in France 19/01/1918.
90. Charles H.E. Manner served in WWI 1914-1918.
91. Private Peter Collins of Ballyboggan awarded a medal for bravery in WWI in 1917.
92. Private John Kelly of Carrick Road decorated in 1917 for rescuing an officer.
93. William Upton Tyrell, Ballindoolin House, fought in WWI and WWII. Injured at the Battle of the Somme, 01/07/1916.
94. E.W. Mather Brookville, Edenderry, died in WWI in 1916.

Appendix 5

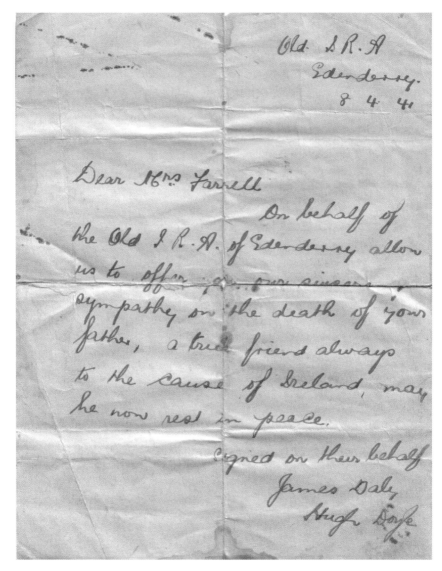

This is a letter in private possession that was sent to the author's grandmother Mrs Mary Farrell (*née* McEvoy) of the Derries, Edenderry, on the
death of her father, William (Bill) McEvoy in April 1941. As a member of the
Irish Volunteers and a member of the IRA during the War of Independence,
William's name is recorded on the IRA memorial in St Mary's Churchyard,
which was erected in 1960.

Endnotes

Introduction

1 *Leinster Leader*, 31 October 1891.
2 *Leinster Leader*, 6 August 1881.
3 In 1975 it was rumoured that the statue was to be removed. See Elgy Gillespie in the *Irish Times*, 5 February 1975.
4 Philip Luckombe, *A Tour Through Ireland: wherein the present state of that Kingdom is considered, and the most noted cities, towns, seats* (Dublin 1780), p.54.
5 John Gough, *Account of two journies southward in Ireland in 1817* (Dublin, 1817), p.46.
6 Charles Coote, *Statistical survey of King's County* (Dublin, 1801), p.121.
7 John Noel McEvoy, 'A study of the United Irish League in King's County 1899-1918', (Unpublished M.A. thesis, NUI Maynooth, 1992).

Agrarian unrest 1820-40

8 WA Maguire (ed.), *Letters of a great Irish Landlord; a selection of estate correspondance of the third marquess of Downshire,* 1809-1845 (Belfast, 1974) pp104-6.
9 *Offaly Topic*, 'Pages From the Past', 8 July 1999.
10 WA Maguire (ed.), *Letters of a great Irish Landlord; a selection of estate correspondance of the third marquess of Downshire,* 1809-1845 (Belfast, 1974), p104.
11 Ibid, p.113.
12 Ibid, p.111.
13 Ibid, p.110.
14 Ibid, pp114-19.
15 Ibid, p.106.
16 *Offaly Topic*, 'Pages From the Past', 8 July 1999.
17 Mairead Evans and Noel Whelan, *Edenderry through the ages* (Edenderry, 2000), p.43.
18 *Offaly Topic*, 'Pages From the Past', 8 July 1999.
19 *The Times*, 7 February 1822.
20 *The Times*, 23 July 1829.
21 G. Slater to Sir C. Saxton, 3 March 1812, in SOC II 162 (1811-12).
22 A. Armstrong to Dublin Castle, 1 November 1819, SOC 2077/ 27.
23 Lieutenant William Henderson, Edenderry to Dublin Castle, 29 April 1824, SOC 2607/2.

24 Printed notice in Edenderry, October 1831, SOC II 177 (1831).

25 Evidence of M.L. Dames, taken before the commissioners appointed to inquire into the occupation of land in Ireland, etc. *(Devon Report) HC* 1845 *xxi* [657], pp 604-5.

26 Notice posted near Edenderry, 21 July 1820, SOC II 169 (1820-21).

27 Report from the King's County, 24 February 1827, SOC 2831/ 18.

28 *The Times*, 1 September 1829.

29 *Carlow Morning Post*, 31 August 1829.

30 WA Maguire (ed.), *Letters of a great Irish Landlord; a selection of estate correspondance of the third marquess of Downshire,* 1809-1845 (Belfast, 1974), p.84.

31 Ibid, p.84.

32 Ibid, p.86.

33 See Ciaran Reilly, *The Downshire Estate, Edenderry Co. Offaly* 1790-1800 (Dublin, 2007).

34 WA Maguire (ed.), *Letters of a great Irish Landlord; a selection of estate correspondance of the third marquess of Downshire,* 1809-1845 (Belfast, 1974), p.79.

35 Petition of the Roman Catholic and Protestant inhabitants of Ballymacwilliam to the House of Lords, 18 July 1831, (P.R.O.N.I., D/ 607/ C/ 12/ 453).

36 Edenderry Historical Society, *The influence of Lord Downshire on the Downshire estate, Edenderry* 1809-1845 (Edenderry, 1996).

37 See Kathy Trant, *The Blessington estate* 1667-1908 (Dublin, 2004), p.92.

38 WA Maguire, *The Downshire estates in Ireland* 1801-1845 (Oxford, 1972).

39 Ibid.

40 Ibid.

41 Ibid.

42 Jonathan Binns, *The Miseries and Beauties of Ireland* (1837 vol II)

43 Edward Kelly to Lord Downshire, 14 August 1837, (P.R.O.N.I., Downshire papers, D/ 607/C/12 /690).

44 Lord Downshire to Mr Manners, 26 November 1818, (P.R.O.N.I., Downshire papers, D/607/ C/12/205).

45 Col Lloyd to Lord Downshire, 2 May 1841 (P.R.O.N.I., Downshire papers, D/607/C/ 12/783).

46 Edward Lucas to Lord Downshire, 1 December 1843, (P.R.O.N.I., Downshire Papers, D/ 607/ C/ 12/ 840).

47 Marquess of Downshire to the Duke of Wellington, 9 March 1841, (P.R.O.N.I., Downshire papers, D/607/ C/12/ 777).

48 Draft letter of the Marquess of Downshire, 9 March 1841, (P.R.O.N.I., Downshire papers, D/ 607/ C/ 12 /776).

The Famine at Edenderry

49 *Leinster Express*, 13 April 1839.

50 Thomas Murray to Lord Downshire, 10 March 1840 (Ms Local history section, Edenderry Public Library).

51 The area was broken down as follows: Kildare (69, 435 acres) Kings County (81, 041 acres) Meath (21, 914 acres).

52 *Leinster Express*, 7 November 1840.

53 *The Times*, 29 July 1843.

54 *The Times*, 21 July 1843.

55 *The Times*, 3 October 1843.

56 *The Times*, 22 September 1841.

57 *Leinster Express*, 22 April 1843.
58 *The Times*, 4 December 1843.
59 *The Nation*, 5 May 1843.
60 Earl of Rosse to Lord Downshire, 29 May 1843, (P.R.O.N.I., Downshire papers, D/607/C/12/842).
61 *The Nation*, 29 July 1843.
62 *The Times*, 25 September 1845.
63 MS material in the Local History section, Edenderry Public Library.
64 *The Times*, 17 October 1846.
65 Brendan O Cathain, *Famine Diary*, (Dublin, 1999).
66 *The Times*, 16 August 1848.
67 *The Times*, 3 December 1849.
68 *King's County Chronicle*, 29 March 1848.

Edenderry 1850-80: industry and development
69 *The Times*, 7 February 1851.
70 *Leinster Leader*, 11 March 1882.
71 *Offaly Topic*, 8 July 1999.
72 *The Times*, 7 January 1916.
73 *The Times*, 11 January 1856.
74 *The Times*, 3 June 1863.
75 *The Times*, 9 July 1870.
76 *The Times*, 10 March 1866.
77 Trade List of the Universal Providing Stores, Edenderry 1899. (Local history section, Edenderry Library).
78 *The Times*, 1 January 1866.
79 *King's County Chronicle*, 10 January 1866.
80 *The Times*, 30 December 1871.
81 Michael Murphy, *Edenderry a Leinster town* (Tullamore, 2004) p.30.
82 *King's County Chronicle*, 15 June 1904.

The Land War and the Edenderry Home Rule club
83 *Leinster Leader*, 6 August 1881.
84 Ibid.
85 *Leinster Leader*, 31 October 1891.
86 *Leinster Leader*, 25 June 1881.
87 *Leinster Leader*, 31 October 1891.
88 List of all persons detained in prison under the Statue Victoria 4, HC 1881 LXXVI.
89 *Leinster Leader*, 25 June 1881.
90 Ibid.
91 Ibid.
92 *Leinster Leader*, 30 July 1881.
93 Ibid.
94 Ibid.
95 Ibid.
96 Ibid.
97 *Leinster Leader*, 6 August 1881.
98 J.W. Carter, *The Land War and its leaders in Queen's County* 1879-82, (Portlaoise, 1994).
99 *Leinster Leader*, 6 August 1881.

100 *Leinster Leader*, 13 August 1881.
101 Ibid.
102 *Leinster Leader*, 26 November 1881.
103 *Leinster Leader*, 12 November 1881.
104 *Leinster Leader*, 26 November 1881.
105 Gerard Moran, 'Political developments in King's County 1868-85', in William Nolan and Timothy P. O'Neill *Offaly history and society: interdisciplinary essays on the history of an Irish county* (Dublin, 1998), p.778.
106 *King's County Chronicle*, 13 January 1876.
107 *Leinster Leader*, 12 November 1881.
108 *The Nation*, 2 September 1876.
109 *The Nation*, 24 September 1877.
110 Gerard Moran, 'Political developments in King's County 1868-85', in William Nolan and Timothy P. O'Neill *Offaly history and society: interdisciplinary essays on the history of an Irish county* (Dublin, 1998), p.781.
111 Ibid.
112 *The Nation*, 8 June 1878.
113 *The Nation*, 28 October 1878.
114 *The Nation*, 22 September 1878.
115 *The Nation*, 3 & 24 September 1878.
116 *King's County Chronicle*, 15, 22 & 29 January 1880.
117 *Leinster Leader*, 11 September 1880.
118 *Leinster Leader*, 17 September 1880.
119 *Leinster Leader*, 19 March 1881.
120 Diary of Garrett Tyrell (1888), MS material at Edenderry Library.
121 Ibid.
122 Ibid.
123 *Leinster Leader*, 12 November 1881.
124 Diary of Garrett Tyrell (1888), MS material at Edenderry Library.
125 *Leinster Leader*, 21 January 1882.
126 Ibid.
127 *Leinster Leader*, 18 May 1883.
128 *Leinster Leader*, 23 April 1881.
129 *Leinster Leader*, 26 March 1881.
130 *Leinster Leader*, 2 April 1881.
131 *Leinster Leader*, 9 June 1883.
132 *Leinster Leader*, 14 July 1883.
133 *Leinster Leader*, 26 May 1883.
134 *Leinster Leader*, 3 November 1883.
135 *Leinster Leader*, 8 November 1884.
136 *Leinster Leader*, 18 October 1884.
137 *Midland Tribune*, 13 August 1885.
138 *Midland Tribune*, 10 September 1885.
139 *Midland Tribune*, 17 September 1885.
140 *Leinster Leader*, 9 January 1886.
141 *Leinster Leader*, 22 November 1884.
142 *Leinster Leader*, 16 January 1886.
143 *Leinster Leader*, 26 February 1886.
144 Ibid.

145 *Leinster Leader*, 12 February 1887.

146 *Leinster Leader*, 23 April 1887.

147 Ibid.

148 *Leinster Leader*, 14 May 1887.

149 *Leinster Leader*, 13 August 1887.

150 *Leinster Leader*, 27 August 1887.

151 James Lydon, *The making of modern Ireland*, (London, 1998).

152 *Leinster Leader*, 10 January 1891.

153 *Leinster Leader*, 3 January 1891.

154 *Leinster Leader*, 21 February 1891.

155 *Leinster Leader,* 26 July 1890.

156 *Leinster Leader*, 24 January 1891.

157 *Leinster Leader*, 31 January 1891.

158 *Leinster Leader*, 28 February 1891.

159 *Leinster Leader*, 7 March 1891.

160 *Leinster Leader*, 20 March 1891.

161 *Leinster Leader*, 31 October 1891.

Literary nationalism and pastimes

162 Dr Philip Brady, *A Place in Poetry*, (Edenderry, 1998).

163 *Leinster Leader*, 24 June 1893.

164 *Leinster Leader*, 17 February 1893.

165 *Irish Weekly Independent*, 4 June 1910.

166 *Irish Weekly Independent*, 14 September 1907.

167 *The Weekly Freeman*, 17 March 1907.

168 *Midland Tribune*, 6 April 1889.

169 *Leinster Leader*, 30 April 1887.

170 *Midland Tribune*, 24 August 1895.

171 *Leinster Leader*, 18 January 1896.

172 *Leinster Express*, 17 May 1986.

173 See Perl W. Morgan, *History of Wyandotte County Kansas and its people* (Chicago, 1911).

174 R. J. Egar, 'Killian, Andrew (1872-1939)', *Australian Dictionary of Biography, Volume* 9, 1983, pp 591-592.

Edenderry Town Council and the decline of Home Rule

175 *The Times*, 23 March 1893.

176 *Leinster Leader*, 6 January 1900.

177 *Leinster Leader*, 10 March 1900.

178 *Westmeath Nationalist*, 14 May 1896.

179 *King's County Council*, 28 May 1891.

180 *Leinster Leader*, 8 April 1898.

181 *Midland Tribune*, 13 May 1899.

182 RIC Crime Branch special précis of information relating to Secret Societies, January 1899-February 1905.

183 CO 904/11/1905-1908: précis of information received by the Special Branch RIC.

184 *Midland Tribune*, 7 September 1901.

185 *The Times*, 1 March 1900.

186 Rory O'Kennedy, 'Effect of the 1898 Local Government Act on King's County' (unpublished essay, Certificate in local history, NUI Maynooth, 1999).

187 *Midland Tribune*, 18 November 1905.
188 Edenderry GAA, *The Tale of the Reds* (Edenderry, 1997), p.18.
189 The Collins Papers, Department of Defence Archives A/ 1063 pos.193 N.L.I.
190 Ibid.

Edenderry men in the 'Great War' 1914-18
191 James Lydon, *The Making of Modern Ireland*, (London, 1998).
192 *Leinster Leader*, 14 April 1917.
193 *Offaly Topic*, 25 April 1991.
194 *Leinster Leader*, 18 March 1916.
195 *Leinster Leader*, 16 April 1916.
196 *Leinster Leader*, 29 April 1916.
197 *Leinster Leader*, 15 July 1916.
198 *Leinster Leader*, 22 July 1916.
199 I am indebted to Ms Antoinette Tyrell for quoting from her paper 'Ballindoolin
    House, Carbury, Co. Kildare', submitted to the NUI Maynooth, Dept. of Modern
    History.
200 *Leinster Leader*, 5 May 1917.
201 *Leinster Leader*, 13 July 1918.
202 *Leinster Leader*, 16 November 1918.

Edenderry in the War of Independence 1916-21
203 CO 904/120/1916: Special report on the state of the counties.
204 *Leinster Leader*, 8 July 1916.
205 *Leinster Leader*, 17 June 1920.
206 *Leinster Leader*, 30 April 1992.
207 *Leinster Leader*, 7 July 1917.
208 *The Times*, 24 March & 31 May 1919.
209 *Leinster Leader*, 3 January 1920.
210 *Leinster Leader*, 10 January 1920.
211 Ibid.
212 *Leinster Leader*, 6 August 1920.
213 *Leinster Leader*, 5 February 1921.
214 *Leinster Leader*, 26 March 1921.
215 *Leinster Leader*, 4 June 1921.
216 Mary Daly, 'From King's county to Offaly: Dáil Éireann and local government during
    the years of the Irish revolution' in Nolan, William; O'Neill, Timothy P. (eds.), *Offaly
    history and society: interdisciplinary essays on the history of an Irish county* (Dublin, 1998),
    pp831–854.
217 *Leinster Leader*, 23 July 1921.
218 *Leinster Leader*, 17 December 1921.
219 *Leinster Leader*, 22 October 1921.
220 *Leinster Leader*, 12 November 1921.

Aftermath: Civil War and compensation
221 *Leinster Leader*, 27 January 1923.
222 *Leinster Leader*, 29 July 1922.
223 *Leinster Leader*, 26 August 1922.
224 *Leinster Leader*, 23 September 1922.
225 *Leinster Leader*, 9 December 1922.

226 Dáil Debates: Volume 6, 10 January 1924. Written Answers/Edenderry Volunteer Payments.

227 Dáil Debates: Volume 7, 13 June 1924. Oral Answers/Edenderry dependants allowance.

228 Dáil Debates: Volume 6, 12 February 1924 Oral Answers Dependents allowance Edenderry.

229 Dáil Debates: Volume 2, 30 January 1923, Written Answers.

230 Dáil Debates: Volume 10, 12 March 1925, Oral Answers.

231 Dáil Debates: Volume 6, 18 January 1924, Written answers.

232 Dáil Debates: Volume 6, 9 April 1924, Oral Answers, Edenderry Army account.

233 Dáil Debates: Volume 7, 9 May 1924, Oral Answers.

234 Dáil Debates: Volume 9, 19 December 1924, Written Answers.

235 FIN 1/1074, N.A.I., Compensation claims of Victimised Loyalists, 6 October 1922.

236 FIN 1/2607, N.A.I., Commandeered Motor Vehicles.

237 Dáil Debates: Volume 6, 11 April 1924, Oral Answers.

238 Dáil Debates: Volume 5, 10 October 1923, Oral Answers.

239 *Leinster Leader*, 27 January 1923.

240 *Leinster Leader*, 3 February 1923.

241 *Leinster Leader*, 14 April 1923.

242 Dáil Éireann Volume 61: 21 March 1936, Oral Answers.

243 Dáil Éireann Volume 38: 21 May 1931, Oral Answers.

244 Dáil Éireann minutes, 1925.

245 *Leinster Leader*, 3 March 1923.

246 See Terence Dooley, *The Decline of the Big House in Ireland* (Dublin, 2001), p.178.

247 *Leinster Leader*, 15 October 1921.

248 Tony Moran, Ballyna Annual 2006 (31st Annual).

Appendices

249 *The Times*, 21 May 1915.

250 Ibid.

251 *Leinster Leader*, 25 May 1918.

252 *Leinster Leader*, 13 July 1918.

253 Ibid.

254 Ibid.

255 *Leinster Leader*, 30 November 1916.

256 *The Times*, 4 December 1917.

257 *Leinster Leader*, 4 March 1916.

258 *Leinster Leader*, 12 August 1916.

259 *Leinster Leader*, 14 April 1917.

260 *Leinster Leader*, 5 May 1917.

261 Vivienne Clarke, *Offaly involvement in World War I*, (Offaly Historical Society, 1984).

262 *Leinster Leader*, 17 March 1900.